Palgrave Studies in Economic History

Series Editor
Kent Deng
London School of Economics
London, UK

Palgrave Studies in Economic History is designed to illuminate and enrich our understanding of economies and economic phenomena of the past. The series covers a vast range of topics including financial history, labour history, development economics, commercialisation, urbanisation, industrialisation, modernisation, globalisation, and changes in world economic orders.

More information about this series at
http://www.palgrave.com/gp/series/14632

Enriqueta Camps-Cura

Changes in Population, Inequality and Human Capital Formation in the Americas in the Nineteenth and Twentieth Centuries

A Comparative Perspective

palgrave
macmillan

Enriqueta Camps-Cura
Pompeu Fabra University
Barcelona, Spain

Palgrave Studies in Economic History
ISBN 978-3-030-21350-3 ISBN 978-3-030-21351-0 (eBook)
https://doi.org/10.1007/978-3-030-21351-0

Cover illustration: imageBROKER/Alamy Stock Photo

This Palgrave Pivot imprint is published by the registered company Springer Nature Switzerland AG
The registered company address is: Gewerbestrasse 11, 6330 Cham, Switzerland

Acknowledgements

This book represents an update of a research project that began years ago, during a nearly two-year long leave (2005–2006) at University of Harvard (Economics Department), thanks to an invitation to visit this university from Jeffrey G. Williamson. My visit to Harvard implied a change of methodology and research goals, from micro history to macro comparative economic history. I am especially indebted to Jeff Williamson, who acted as an excellent mentor, as well as to many other participants of the Economic Development Seminar led by him. Among them I am particularly indebted to Stanley Engerman, with whom I reprised intellectual collaboration years later and who coauthored with me the papers behind three of the chapters presented in this book.

I also must acknowledge research assistants at Univeritat Pompeu Fabra, for helping me to obtain and update datasets and also to obtain results. My most sincere gratitude to Thomas Woickzyk, Ana Rodríguez González, and Christina Hans for their excellent work, sometimes with close deadlines and difficult research questions.

Many other academics have helped me at Unviersitat Pompeu Fabra, allowing to spend long leaves at other universities and discussing with me contents and approaches of my research over the long run. In this respect I am particularly indebted to Albert Carreras de Odriozola and I also want to stress help by Andreu Mas-Colell who made my dream to visit Harvard a reality.

Last but not least, I received excellent suggestions from two anonymous referees as well as from Professor Deng from LSE, director of this collection. Palgrave Macmillan offered me renewed chances to finish this book, partially written during an intensive teaching period.

To all of them my most sincere gratitude,
Enriqueta Camps-Cura

Contents

1 **Introduction: Population Growth and the Debate on Income and Human Capital Inequality in the Americas in the Long Run—A Comparative Analysis** 1
Bibliography 6

2 **The Impact of Race and Inequality on Human Capital Formation in Latin America During Nineteenth and Twentieth Centuries** 9
Introduction 10
The Development of the Educational System 10
Education and Inequality 16
Inequality, Education and Race 18
Conclusion 26
Bibliography 27

3 **Education and Inequality in North America in the Long Term with Special Reference to the United States** 31
The Summary of the Empirical Evidence 37
Data Sources and Methodology 37

The Time Series on Human Capital, Real Wages, and GDP Per Capita During the Twentieth Century 38
Bibliography 40

4 **World Population Growth and Fertility Patterns, 1960–2010: A Simple Model Explaining the Evolution of the World's Fertility—The Americas in a Comparative Framework** 41
Introduction 42
Are Demographic Patterns Converging Across the World? 44
A Simple Model of the Reasons for Declining Fertility 49
The Empirical Results on Variables Affecting Fertility 52
Conclusion 57
Bibliography 59

5 **The Economic Geography of Human Capital in Twentieth-Century Latin America in an International Comparative Perspective** 61
Introduction 62
Data Sources and Methodology 65
The Evolution of Human Capital During the Twentieth Century in Quantitative Terms 65
The Role of Race and Ethnicity in Educational Attainment 69
Latin America's Education Attainment in an International Comparative Perspective 75
Conclusions 79
Appendix 80
Bibliography 84

6 **Education and Children's Work: Spain, Latin America, and Developing Countries** 87
Introduction: The Human Capital Transition 88
A Model of the Transition to the Human Capital Century in Spain 89
The Data 92

The Historical Evidence from Catalonia as a Spanish Case Study 92
Human Capital and Children's Work in Current Developing Countries 94
Conclusion 104
Bibliography 105

7 **Education, Gender Gap, and Market Openness: A Comparative Study of Urban Latin America and East Asia (1970–2000)** 109
Introduction 110
The Data 113
The Methodology 116
Real Income Versus Human Capital Gender GAP 118
A Micro Analysis of the Gendered Wage Rates 122
Conclusions 127
Bibliography 128

8 **Income and Human Capital Inequality and Ethnicity in the Americas During the Second Era of Globalization (1960–2010)** 133
Introduction 134
Data Sources and Methodology 136
Results on Ethnicity, Education, and Economic Growth 136
Results on Ethnicity, Inequality, and Sector of Employment 141
Bibliography 154

Index 157

List of Figures

Fig. 2.1	Years of schooling of population aged 15 or more in the six biggest countries of Latin America, 1870–2010	13
Fig. 2.2	Illiteracy rates in Latin America in the six biggest countries, 1920–2000	14
Fig. 2.3	Educational and income inequality in Latin America, 1850–2000	17
Fig. 3.1	GDP per capita and real wages in the US, 1900–2000	38
Fig. 3.2	Life expectancy, years of schooling and real wages in the US, 1900–2000	39
Fig. 3.3	GDP per capita and real wages in Canada, 1900–2000	39
Fig. 3.4	Life expectancy, years of schooling and real wages in Canada, 1900–2000	40
Fig. 4.1	Fertility rates in the world regions, 1960–2000	46
Fig. 4.2	Infant mortality rates in the world regions, 1960–2000	47
Fig. 4.3	A model on the variables affecting fertility	50
Fig. 4.4	The gender gap in infant mortality rates, 2000	57
Fig. 5.1	Illiteracy rates in the regions of Latin America, 1900–2000	66
Fig. 5.2	Years of schooling in the regions of Latin America, 1900–2000	66

Fig. 5.3 Educational Inequality in the regions of Latin America, 1900–2000 67
Fig. 5.4 Evolution of average years of education applying Diff-in-Diff model 72
Fig. 5.5 Primary schooling in the regions of Latin America, 1950–2000 76
Fig. 5.6 Secondary schooling in the regions of Latin America, 1950–2000 76
Fig. 5.7 Average years in university in the regions of Latin America, 1950–2000 77
Fig. 5.8 Height in the regions of Latin America, 1900–2000 77
Fig. 5.9 Life expectancies in the regions of Latin America, 1900–2000 78
Fig. 5.10 GDP per capita in the regions of Latin America, 1900–2000 78
Fig. 6.1 Women's real wages and fertility evolution: the Catalan case, 1900–1935 93
Fig. 6.2 Child labour and GDP per capita in the developing world 96
Fig. 6.3 Life expectancy and GDP, developing world 97
Fig. 6.4 The U shaped female labor participation function in development. World wide sample, 2000 97
Fig. 6.5 The influence of children's work on infant mortality. World wide sample, 2000 98
Fig. 6.6 The influence of female labor participation in infant mortality. World wide sample, 2000 98
Fig. 6.7 The relationship between the gender gap (income female/ income male) and economic inequality 99
Fig. 6.8 The relationship between children's work and economic inequality 99
Fig. 6.9 Years of schooling on adult women in the biggest countries of Latin America (1960–2000) 102
Fig. 6.10 Child labor force participation in the biggest countries of Latin America (1960–2000) 102
Fig. 6.11 Children's work as a function of women's earnings. World wide sample, 2000–2003 103
Fig. 6.12 The gender gap. World countries, 2003 104
Fig. 8.1 Income inequality and white population (American countries, 1960–2005) 142

Fig. 8.2	Income inequality and white population (American countries, 1960–2005)	143
Fig. 8.3	Educational inequality and white population (American countries, 1960–2005)	143
Fig. 8.4	Educational inequality and white population (American countries, 1960–2005)	144
Fig. 8.5	Income inequality and Indian population (American countries, 1960–2005)	144
Fig. 8.6	Income inequality and Indian population (American countries, 1960–2005)	145
Fig. 8.7	Educational inequality and Indian population (American countries, 1960–2005)	145
Fig. 8.8	Educational inequality and Indian population (American countries, 1960–2005)	146
Fig. 8.9	Income inequality and black or mixed population (American countries, 1960–2005)	146
Fig. 8.10	Income inequality and black or mixed population (American countries, 1960–2005)	147
Fig. 8.11	Educational inequality and black or mixed population (American countries, 1960–2005)	147
Fig. 8.12	Educational inequality and black or mixed population (American countries, 1960–2005)	148
Fig. 8.13	Agricultural sector and black or mixed population (American countries, 1960–2005)	148
Fig. 8.14	Agricultural sector and black or mixed population (American countries, 1960–2005)	149
Fig. 8.15	Industrial sector and black or mixed population (American countries, 1960–2005)	149
Fig. 8.16	Industrial sector and black or mixed population (American countries, 1960–2005)	150
Fig. 8.17	Services sector and black or mixed population (American countries, 1960–2005)	150
Fig. 8.18	Services sector and black or mixed population (American countries, 1960–2005)	151
Fig. 8.19	Agricultural sector and Indian population (American countries, 1960–2005)	151
Fig. 8.20	Agricultural sector and Indian population (American countries, 1960–2005)	152

Fig. 8.21 Industrial sector and Indian population (American countries, 1960–2005) 152
Fig. 8.22 Industrial sector and Indian population (American countries, 1960–2005) 153
Fig. 8.23 Services sector and Indian population (American countries, 1960–2005) 153
Fig. 8.24 Services sector and Indian population (American countries, 1960–2005) 154

Map 7.1 The earnings gender gap at the world level, 2003 114

List of Tables

Table 1.1	GDP per capita (weighted by population)	5
Table 2.1	Ethnicity, in 1825, and literacy	11
Table 2.2	Average years of schooling according to income deciles, 1990s	19
Table 2.3	The impact of race on years of schooling in 1960	21
Table 2.4	The impact of race on years of schooling in 2000	21
Table 2.5	The impact of race on educational inequality (educational gini) in 1960	22
Table 2.6	The impact of race on educational inequality (educational gini) in 2000	22
Table 2.7	Part I	23
Table 2.7	Part II	24
Table 2.7	Part III	25
Table 2.7	Part IV	26
Table 4.1a	Mean fertility by region, 1960 (births/women at reproductive age)	47
Table 4.1b	Mean fertility by region, 2010	48
Table 4.2a	Mean infant mortality rates by region, 1960 (deaths of children younger than one/births)	48
Table 4.2b	Mean infant mortality rates by region, 2010	48
Table 4.3	Mortality and Race; twentieth century US	49

Table 4.4	The variables affecting fertility at the world level, 1965–2010	53
Table 4.5	Explaining the gender gap, 2003	56
Table 5.1	Race, education and GDP per capita	71
Table 5.2	Race, education and GDP per capita	71
Table 5.3	Primary schooling laws and education—Diff-in-Diff	73
Table 5.4	Education and GDP per capita—IV results	74
Table 5.5	Year 2000	80
Table 5.6	Year 1950	80
Table 5.7	Year 1900	81
Table 5.8	Elasticities of GDP per capita with respect to the average years of schooling	81
Table 5.9	Year 2000	81
Table 5.10	Year 1950	82
Table 5.11	Year 1960	82
Table 5.12	Results weighted by population size	83
Table 5.13	Year 1950	83
Table 6.1	Explaining children's work in nowadays developing countries. An across country panel linear regression, 1960–2000	100
Table 6.2	The influence of social capital in per capita GDP	101
Table 7.1	The use of work time according to gender in poor countries, 1990–2000 (unweighted averages)	119
Table 7.2	The role of market openness and culture in shaping the human capital gender gap	121
Table 7.3	Inequality and gender in urban Latin America and East Asia	123
Table 7.4	Gender gap evolution and dissimilarity index in a sample of urban Asian and Latin American countries, 1975–1995	124
Table 7.5	Female economic activity. World indicators	125
Table 7.6	Female literacy. World indicators, 2003	125
Table 8.1	GDP per capita and ethnicity (1960)	137
Table 8.2	GDP per capita and ethnicity (2000)	138
Table 8.3	Average years of education and ethnicity (1960)	139
Table 8.4	Average years of education and ethnicity (2000)	140
Table 8.5	Average GDP per capita growth (1960–2010) by ethnic composition	140

1

Introduction: Population Growth and the Debate on Income and Human Capital Inequality in the Americas in the Long Run—A Comparative Analysis

Abstract In this introductory chapter, we introduce the most relevant bibliography on the main questions regarding income inequality and human capital in the Americas in the long run, as well as the demographic trends of the period outlined in Chapter 4. The chapter deals with the very different origins and evolution of income and human capital inequality in Latin America with respect to North America, specially the United States. A lot of available information dates the origins of Latin American inequality in the colonial period (Engerman and Sokoloff 2012; Acemoglu et al. 2011; Acemoglu and Robinson 2012; Berola and O'Campo 2013). Iberian colonizers dealt with the distribution of production factors in South America in a more unequal way than North European colonizers in North America. But Williamson (2010, 2015) argue on a different perspective stressing that levels on income per capita in Latin America were too low to allow for high levels of inequality.

Keywords: Inequality · Human capital · Colonial origins · Great Leveling · Comparative

E. Camps-Cura, *Changes in Population, Inequality and Human Capital Formation in the Americas in the Nineteenth and Twentieth Centuries*, Palgrave Studies in Economic History,
https://doi.org/10.1007/978-3-030-21351-0_1

The extent to which Latin America was one of the most unequal continents of the world during the last 5 centuries has been a matter of debate in recent literature. After the arrival of Spanish colonizers in 1492 this continent, during the sixteenth and seventeenth centuries, indigenous population suffered from high epidemic mortality and around 80% died (Livi-Bacci 2006). This fact and a demographic regime characterized by low population densities implied that natural resources were abundant at the per capita level. The Malthusian hypothesis born from European overpopulation never operated in this context. In this framework of low demographic pressure and abundance of natural resources the main activities were organized in the form of big mining or agrarian firms. During the late nineteenth-century world globalization period the continent specialized in the exports of products such as sugar, cocoa, coffee, cattle, and other mining products demanded by the European urbanization and the industrial revolution. All these products enjoyed large economies of scale and therefore the optimal way to produce them was in the form of big firms and plantations. The high levels of property concentration were therefore a characteristic feature of the economy of the continent in the period under consideration (Engerman and Sokoloff 2012; Camps 2013).

In a recent paper on world's trends of wellbeing inequality in the long run Prados de la Escosura (2018) states that while in terms of income there was an increase of inequality until the third quarter of the twentieth century, in terms of human capital (health and education) inequality fell since World War I. In this book, we present the results based on some of the data on inequality built by Prados de la Escosura (2007) for the Americas.

Engerman and Sokoloff (2012) have stressed that the aforementioned economic picture of high levels of property concentration reinforces the hypothesis that levels of income inequality were high since the colonial period and afterwards. The high levels of concentration of factor endowments, land and labor, exogenous factors of the production function, implied the very unequal distribution of income. Furthermore the economic institutions created to afford transaction costs in this context perpetuated economic inequality. According to these authors the main institutions were those dealing with education, land property, and political rights such as the right to vote. In sharp contrast with the United States were soon a dense network of public schools depending on the local governments were created in Latin America the educational institutions were financed by the central government and were addressed to educate the children of the colonial elites. We already mentioned that land property was concentrated in a few hands. Regarding the right to vote only the literate population could make use of it. And we already mentioned that the education supply was restricted to the children of the colonial elites. Both endowments and institutions were responsible for the high levels of inequality reached in Latin America, according to these authors.

Acemoglu et al. (2011) and Acemoglu and Robinson (2012) also stress the different role of institutions in North and South America when explaining the sharp contrast in the levels of welfare and wellbeing attained in both parts of the continent. While in North America inclusive and democratic institutions prevailed since the colonization era, in Latin America institutions were and continue to be extractive. This different nature of the institutions explain according to the authors the different levels of wellbeing and welfare in both parts of the Americas up to the present and have their origins in the colonization period.

Contrasting with Engerman and Sokoloff, Williamson (2010, 2015) argues that in the first centuries of the colonial period the levels of per capita GDP of Latin American societies were too low to generate enough surplus that could be extracted by the elites causing high levels of inequality and that therefore by then levels of inequality were low, and not higher than those of Europe, North America, and other continents. Since levels of income in Latin America were lower than those of the European metropolis, the extraction rate and inequality levels were also lower. His hypothesis is that Latin American levels of inequality increased later during the seventeenth and eighteenth centuries, as measured by Gini coefficients, but they were not higher than those of the European metropolis. Therefore high levels of inequality were not a characteristic feature of Latin America. According to this author, levels of inequality only increased later, after the 1870s, because of the first world globalization wave that was made possible by the transport revolution. Overpopulation in Europe caused by the demographic transition fostered an important immigration inflow in the Americas, North and South. The huge migration movements changed the preexisting balance of production factors. Immigration implied the increase of the labor supply and therefore the trend of real wages to diminish. On the other hand, a more intensive use of land and the increase of its demand caused an upward trend in the value of rents. The wage/rental ratio decreased as a result of these global movements of production factors and this caused the increase of inequality levels that reached a maximum by this period. But this was caused by market forces and was made possible by the transports revolution (Hatton and Williamson 1998). Afterwards, according to Williamson (2015), Latin America missed the twentieth-century leveling trend which was apparent in North America and in capitalist societies during the Golden Age. It was this fact and not the colonial heritage that resulted in relative higher levels of inequality in LAC. As a result of this aforementioned trend, Latin America was the continent with the highest inequality by the end of the twentieth century.

On the other hand, Coatsworth (2008) stands those levels of inequality in Latin America were not high enough to produce a process of sustained economic growth. The metropolis, Spain, was a backward nation and was unable to protect the interests and property rights of the colonial elites with the required vigor. Land ownership did not receive enough support and was subject to turn over. The institutional reforms necessary to foster an economic spurt (such as the reform of the civil, the commercial and mining codes) arrived late, several decades after independence. According to this author the rise of inequality caused by the first globalization boon after the 1870s was a good incentive for economic growth and existing economic inequality and unequal institutions positively stimulated industrialization during the ISI period.

Finally Bértola and Ocampo (2013) in an illuminating quantitative essay on the economies of the Southern Cone reconciles some of the points of view exposed till now. While the nature of inequality reveals the influences of the colonial heritage during the first globalization period, in the years 1870–1920, inequalities between countries increased. The inside a country inequality also increased because of the reinforced position of the elites over the production system. In spite of the stimulus of the international export markets there was not a movement toward industrialization and technological change and productive specialization was addressed to the exploitation of natural resources with very little stimulus to innovate. This export-led process of economic growth collapsed during the interwar international economic crisis illuminating the limits of the Latin American path to economic growth.

In Table 1.1, we report levels on per capita GDP at the world comparative level to compare Latin American and the US performance with that of other continents. We can observe in the table the process of sustained growth in the United States while the trend of Latin America to grow is weaker. After 1870 Latin America shows a shy trend to grow during the decades of export-led growth. Another period of exceptional growth are the years of Import Substitution Industrialization truncated by the debt crisis of the 1880s but recovers soon and by the end of the twentieth century the trend to growth is visible again. While Latin American economic growth was small in magnitude, widening the gaps with respect to the rich countries of Western Europe and the United States, it was not the worst of the world. The economic performance of most Asian countries before the last decades of the twentieth century and African countries has been worst. With the turn of the century, during the first decades of the twenty-first century the situation of some Latin American and Asian countries changed but this is not our focus of attention here.

Table 1.1 GDP per capita (weighted by population)

Region	1870 (in $)	1900 (in $)	1950 (in $)	2000 (in $)
Africa	1245.021		1801.91	3491.152
Asia (without Japan)	757.4845	773.0493	891.5263	5158.133
Canada	2866	4924	12333	38108
Japan	1160	1856	3023	32988
Latin America	1203.353	1692.199	4243.425	10893.11
USA	3736	6252	15241	45887
Western Europe	3677.039	5279.834	8284.789	35288.11

Real GDP per capita in 2011 US$, 2011 benchmark
Source http://www.ggdc.net/maddison, Prados de la Escosura (2015)

From the discussion presented till now and the per capita GDP evolution evidence we can conclude that the economic structure of Latin America during the nineteenth and twentieth centuries did not foster economic growth. The explanations presented here according to several authors seem to be complementary to understand this trend. Economic inequality and the institutions to deal with it reinforced the structure of an economy based in the agrarian and the mining sector in which only the economic elites were given the economic, political, and educational backgrounds to deal with economic development. These elites had their origins in Spain, a backward country during the nineteenth and twentieth centuries, and they were not able to successfully transform the Latin American economy and produce a catching up process with the countries where the economic spurt caused by the industrial revolution took place. The very different nature of colonization in South and North America is also visible by their respective economic development performance. While the aforementioned institutions, access to land, education, and right to vote had a democratic nature in the United States they excluded the majority of the population in Latin America. During the ISI period, Latin America experienced growth but it was soon truncated by the foreign debt default in the 1980s. Of course, other previous colonies from Asia and Africa had an even worse performance. But part of the countries of these continents was decolonized much later, after the end of World War II.

Bibliography

Acemoglu, D., Johnson, S., Robinson, J.A., "The Colonial Origins of Comparative Development: An Empirical Investigation", *The American Economic Review*, 91, no. 5 (2011): 1369–1401.

Acemoglu, D., Robinson, J.A., *Why Nations Fail: The Origins of Power, Prosperity and Poverty*. New York, Crown Business, 2012.

Bértola, L., Ocampo, J.A., *El desarrollo económico de América Latina desde la Independencia*. México, Fondo de Cultura Economica, 2013.

Camps, E., *Historia Económica Mundial. La formación de la economía internacional* (siglos XVI–XX). Madrid, McGraw-Hill, 2013.

Coatsworth, J.H. "Inequality, Institutions and Economic Growth in Latin America", *Journal of Latin American Studies*, 40, no. 3 (2008): 545–569.

Engerman, S.L., Sokoloff, K.L., *Economic Development in the Americas Since 1500. Endowments and Institutions*. New York, Cambridge University Press and NBER, 2012.

Hatton, T., Williamson, J.G., *The Age of Mass Migration: Causes and Economic Impact*. New York, Oxford University Press, 1998.

Livi-Bacci, M. "The Depopulation of Hispanic America After the Conquest", *Population and Development Review*, 32 (2006): 199–232.

Prados de la Escosura, L., "Inequality and Poverty in Latin America: A Long-Run Exploration", in *The New Comparative Economic History*, edited by T. Hatton, K. O'Rourke, A.M. Taylor. Cambridge, MA, MIT Press, 2007, pp. 291–315.

Prados de la Escosura, L., "World Human Development: 1870–2007", *Review of Income and Wealth*, 61, no. 2 (2015): 220–247.

Prados de la Escosura, L., "Well-Being Inequality in the Long Run", Discussion Paper Series DP12920, Economic History, CEPR, 2018.

Williamson, J.G., "Five Centuries of Latin American Inequality", *Revista de Historia Económica, Journal of Iberian and Latin American Economic History*, 28, no. 2 (2010): 227–252.

Williamosn, J.G., "Latin American Inequality: Colonial Origins, Commodity Booms or a Missed Twentieth Century Leveling?", *Journal of Human Development and Capabilities*, 16, no. 3 (2015): 324–341.

2

The Impact of Race and Inequality on Human Capital Formation in Latin America During Nineteenth and Twentieth Centuries

Abstract In this chapter we present long-run results on education and educational inequality in Latin America. We analyze the reasons behind the delay of the spread of education in this continent and its relationship with income inequality and race. While the racial composition of the population was behind the low literacy levels obtained during the nineteenth and first part of the twentieth centuries, racial inequality and its impact on education and educational inequality decreased during the last decades of the twentieth century. Nonetheless educational levels lagged behind those of the OECD countries even during the late twentieth century. We also find that the spread of primary and to a lesser extent secondary school during the twentieth century can explain the sharp decrease of educational inequality during the same time period. Nonetheless this diminution of educational inequality did not have any impact on the diminution of income inequality at least during the twentieth century.

Keywords Race · Ethnicity · Mass education · Literacy · Estado Docente

E. Camps-Cura, *Changes in Population, Inequality and Human Capital Formation in the Americas in the Nineteenth and Twentieth Centuries*, Palgrave Studies in Economic History,
https://doi.org/10.1007/978-3-030-21351-0_2

Introduction

The recent trends in income inequality in Latin America are generally agreed upon. There was an increase in inequality measured by the Gini coefficient from 1870 to 1990, followed more recently with some decline in inequality after 1990s. An extensive literature has analyzed this topic and its relationship to its colonial origins (Williamson 2010, 2015; Coatsworth 2008; Bertola et al. 2010; Engerman and Sokoloff 2012; Acemoglu et al. 2011; Acemoglu and Robinson 2006; Allen et al. 2015). But in this paper we do not concentrate on this abundant literature on income inequality, but rather in its relationship with other variables such as education and ethnicity and race. We know that the colonial heritage normally implied that literacy was limited in scope to the colonial Spanish elite (Engerman and Sokoloff 2012).[1] But the analysis of the development of the educational system and the evolution of educational inequality and its impact on income inequality needed further research. This paper tries to study these topics as well as trends in inequality according to ethnic group.

The Development of the Educational System

According to Engerman and Sokoloff (2012) during the nineteenth century education was mainly restricted to those in the white minority of colonial origins, the same as the access to other institutions such as land ownership and political participation. In Table 2.1, we present some preliminary information about the literacy rates in a sample of countries and regions, and compare them with the racial composition of the population.

During the Nineteenth century, literacy rates were low in all Latin American countries, between one-tenth and one-quarter. In all countries education was greater in urban than in rural areas. In the nations in Table 2.1 the proportion of non-whites was over seventy percent. This high proportion of non-whites, and the generally very low level of their education, influences the national average and helps to explain the low

Table 2.1 Ethnicity, in 1825, and literacy

(Who can read and write), selected years			
Country	% Blacks and Native Americans 1825	Literacy rate (%)	
Mexico	81.9	22.2	(1900)
Central America	82.3	11.3	(1893)
Colombia	78.3	–	
Peru and Chile	81.0	13.33	(1854)
Venezuela	74.0	–	
Brazil	81.5	15.8	(1872)

Sources Data on race come from Rosenblat (1945) and data on literacy come from Newland (1991)

level of literacy achieved. Thus, even at the end of the nineteenth century there had to be a major expansion of the educational system to satisfy the educational needs of the largest part of the population.

After the achievement of independence by the Latin American nations in the first decades of the nineteenth century, several countries debated the introduction of reforms of the educational system, and in a few cases, reforms were introduced, in order to guarantee more universal access to primary education. These reforms generally date from the mid-nineteenth century, occurred several years later in Argentina (1884) and Colombia (1886). In the short-run, however, none of these reforms were successful, since the conservative parties leading the reform process wanted mainly to preserve the privileges of the colonial elite and to keep large sectors of the population, mainly the rural and the non-white, marginalized. This initial reform movement aimed at more universal literacy, but was limited in scope and accomplishment during the second half of the nineteenth century (Reimers 2006).

The Catholic church, in contrast with the Protestant church, also played a role in increasing inequality, being generally against the spread of secular education. The Catholic clergy did not support the practice of reading the Bible by laymen and did not regard literacy as a prerequisite for understanding and adhering to Christian values. Literacy was part of the privileges of the clergy and the nobility, and the church perceived education as part of its traditional domain and feared loosening its monopoly control over a privileged medium to spread religious ideology and maintain religious authority (Frankema 2009; Reimers 2006; Landes 1998).

Lindert (2010) demonstrated the relation between the concentration of political power and wealth and low levels of education. According to results by Frankema (2009) (see also Bertola and Ocampo 2013) Latin American countries had lower levels of education than those of some European countries, North America, and Japan, with roughly similar levels of per capita GDP in the years from 1870 to 1930, although the differences within its regions were notable. Argentina, Chile, and Costa Rica were above the Latin American average, while Brazil, Guatemala, and Peru were below the average. This anomaly (LACs lower enrolment rates than could be expected on the bases of their GDP per capita levels) has been attributed by Lindert to the resistance of wealthy social classes to pay taxes to finance the education of the poor. The social elites wanted to maintain their privileges, and were also against a system of direct and progressive taxation. Therefore they were very reluctant to finance the costs of mass primary education aimed at the less favored social classes.

There were, however, marked intra-regional differences in the scale and scope of the diffusion of education in LACs. Countries starting the process of diffusion of mass education earliest were those in the colonial periphery, where the impact of the Iberian metropolis was lower than in the central areas of the colonial system. Countries such as Argentina, Uruguay, and Costa Rica shared some features such as being more urbanized, having higher degrees of ethnic homogeneity, and receiving more migration from Europe and its rural population was more equal. Countries where mass education arrived later were those less urbanized, the rural society was more stratified, with high ethnic heterogeneity and a small white elite. Most of LACs were in between the two extremes and began to invest in mass education at the beginning of the twentieth century (Frankema 2009; Bertola and Ocampo 2013).

Figure 2.1 presents data on the changes in the average years of schooling in the six major economies of Latin America: Argentina, Brazil, Chile, Colombia, Mexico, and Venezuela, in the years from 1880 to 2010. Figure 2.1 has been obtained using the data on average years of schooling

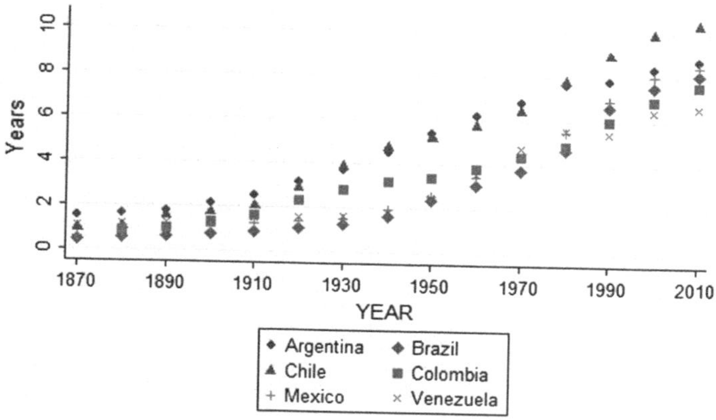

Fig. 2.1 Years of schooling of population aged 15 or more in the six biggest countries of Latin America, 1870–2010 (*Source* Clio Infra)

of the population aged 15 year or more as reported by Clio Infra, a data collection project leaded by Jan Luiten Van Zanden. Note that at the start the average years of schooling was only about one. The percentage of the population with zero years of schooling was high, which greatly reduced the mean years of schooling of the total population. After the start of the twentieth century, all nations began a continuous increase that persisted throughout the century, though even as late 2010, the gap between the highest and lowest educated countries was still about 4 years.

Figure 2.2 presents data on the illiteracy rates of the six countries from 1920 to 2000. Data from Fig. 2.2 are also based in Clio Infra. Illiteracy rates in 1920 were still high, above fifty percent in Colombia, Brazil, Mexico, and Venezuela, and between 30 and 40% in the most southern nations, Argentina and Chile, the two countries with the highest number of years of schooling (see Fig. 2.1). These latter two countries had the highest proportion of white population and received the most immigrants from Europe. This helps to explain the lower rates of illiteracy, since unlike the pattern in the United States, in Latin America the immigrant population tended to be more educated and literate than were the native-born. From 1920 to 2000, all six nations experienced a sharp, continuous decline in the extent of illiteracy, all being below twenty percent by 2010, with Brazil being the nation with the greatest percent of illiterates.

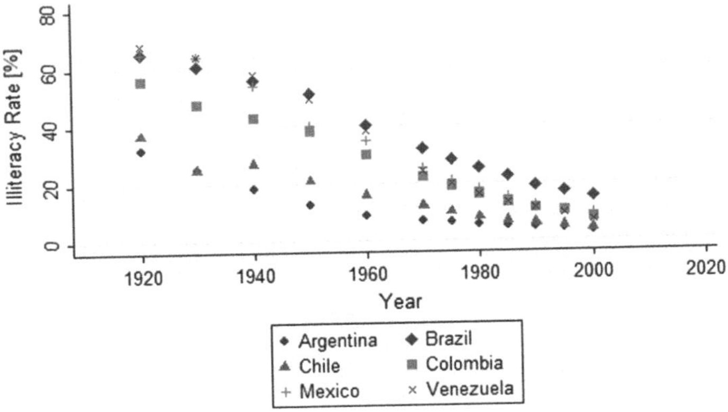

Fig. 2.2 Illiteracy rates in Latin America in the six biggest countries, 1920–2000 (*Source* MOxLAD 2014)

During the twentieth century, due to the confluence of several factors, LACs governments began to support the development of mass education: the need to modernize society and to prepare it with the human capital needed to increase labor productivity; the need to develop national identities; and the need to transform the structure of economic opportunities and to stimulate upward social mobility. This process was controversial because of the different interests of the political parties competing for power, whose discussions of the goals to be attained were based on arguments such as who had the right to education and how, the duration and sponsorship of mandatory primary schooling, and who should have the right to achieve secondary and university education. During the first half of the twentieth century the national systems of public mass education that started during the last part of the nineteenth century was consolidated and there was a growing centralization of educational governance. Conservatives accepted public mandatory primary school with the condition it would not influence social mobility. As we will see the result was the segmentation of the educational system and children from the poor social strata received an education of lower quality with less access to secondary and university school. But the new public system of "Estado Docente" represented an attempt to spread education not only to the elite but to the marginalized populations of blacks, Native-Americans, and mixed non-whites in rural areas. During the years of Import Substitution Industrialization and the period of "Desarrollismo" in the 1950s a modernizing ideology expanded through all Latin America, with liberal parties taking the lead in providing the human capital needed for nascent industries as well as supplying an education to the entire population as inspired by the principles of democracy and human rights.

The influences of this more liberal education policy was truncated, however, in the 1960s with the advent of dictatorships. These dictators abolished the more liberal and democratic aspects of education and demobilized many of the more radical groups that began during "Desarrollismo". They emphasized the development of the necessary skills and knowledge to have workers successfully working in the industrial sector and to further economic growth (Reimers 2006).

This process of reforms came together with changes in the duration of the mandatory public school from 5 or 6 years at the beginning of the twentieth century to 8 or 9 years at the end. More specifically by the end of the twentieth century in the countries reported in Fig. 2.1 the duration of primary school was 9 years in Argentina and Chile, 10 years in Mexico, 8 years in Brazil and Colombia and 7 years in Venezuela. From the results presented in Figs. 2.1 and 2.2 we can conclude that in most of the cases the improvement observed in the average years of schooling and the diminution of illiteracy meant only finishing the primary level of education. According to recent results by Barro and Lee (2013) for the aggregate of LACs by 2010 34.5% of the population aged 15 or more had only attended primary school and 22.3% had completed it, 45.1% had attended secondary school and 25.3% had completed it, and 12.6% had attended tertiary education and 7.1% had completed it. According to the same authors Latin America together with Subsaharan Africa were among the continents of the world where the rates of return to an additional year of schooling were the lowest.

Both Frankema (2009) and Reimers (2006) have argued that the process of expansion of the quantity of education was detrimental to its quality. Frankema has stressed that the average number of schooling years does not inform us about the dropouts and the repetition of grades by many children in the rural areas. By the end of the twentieth century dropouts were higher for the poor families in both the urban and rural settings. In rural areas however there were more children who never attended school (6% in rural areas vs. 1.7% in urban areas) and more dropouts (23% in rural areas vs. 11% in urban). Reimers (2006) informs us about other qualitative variables: high percentages of children in the third- and fourth-grades of a rural primary school report not having a language textbook as opposed to the greater proportion in private schools in urban areas; around 30% of children in all settings did not trust their teachers and constantly fought with classmates; and about 40% of children in the third- and fourth-grades in rural and urban settings report they did not always understand the explanations given by their teachers. Therefore the segmentation of the educational system is apparent and a high proportion of children do not fully profit from the process of reform taking place during the twentieth century. Although the basic level of education for most of the population had increased relatively rapidly during the twentieth century, the gap with respect to the OECD countries remained basically unchanged even during the second half of the century. In order to compete economically with the OECD nations, the educational system still needed marked improvements in both quantity and quality of schooling.

Education and Inequality

As pointed out, education in Latin America was quite unequally distributed among the population in the nineteenth century, and while it became more widely diffused in the twentieth century there remained significant differences within the population, by ethnicity, income level, and rural-urban location. In this section we wish to present some measures of trends in educational inequality as well as in income inequality to examine the extent to which inequality in access to education was related to income inequality.

To measure educational inequality we use the educational Ginis available in the latest Clio Infra. Data on income inequality comes from the published works of Leandro Prados de la Escosura (2007) who provides a series of income Ginis since the middle of the nineteenth century. There is information available based on wage rates (Fitzgerald 2008; Astorga et al. 2005) and on measures of overall income (Coatsworth 2008; Williamson 2010, 2015; Bértola et al. 2010; Arroyo-Abad 2013). Prados de la Escosura offers the longest series, from 1850 to 1990, prepared in a consistent manner, unlike the others which provide evidence for only part of the period. We have added estimates to the series from 1990 to 2000 with the use of official data from the World Bank. While there may be differences in some cases between the estimates of Prados de la Escosura and other sources, these do not lead to any substantial differences, so for reasons of consistency we choose to rely on the Prados de la Escosura estimates.

Figure 2.3 demonstrates that the educational Ginis was high, between 60 and 80, at the end of the nineteenth century, but they trended downward in the twentieth century. The broadening of education appears to

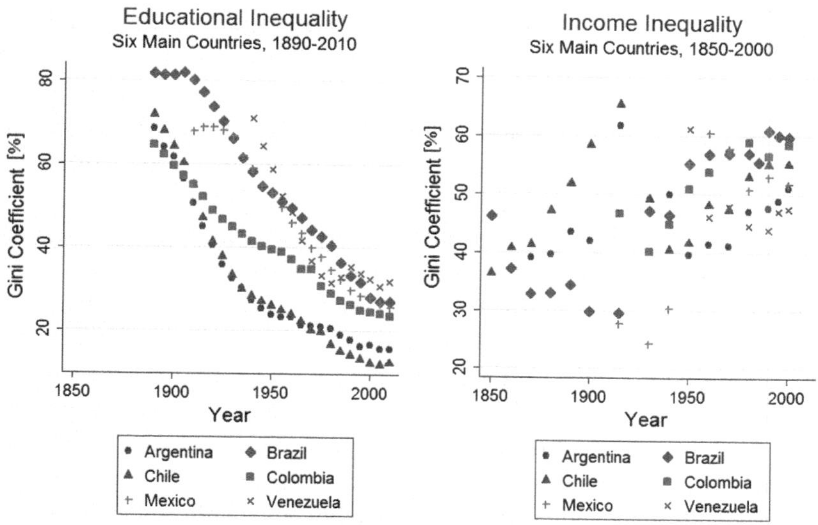

Fig. 2.3 Educational and income inequality in Latin America, 1850–2000 (*Sources* Clio Infra; Prados de la Escosura [2007])

have played a major role in the decline of the educational Ginis, as did the increase of schooling for women (Reimers 2006). The high educational Ginis at the end of the nineteenth century can help to explain why income inequality was so high at this time. Recent studies of the United States during the twentieth century (Goldin and Katz 2008) indicate that the rising returns to education explain part of the rising income levels, suggesting that the unequal distribution of education in nineteenth century Latin America was another important factor in explaining the persistence of high-income inequality.

The widespread declining level of the educational Ginis after 1900 was influenced by the changes in education resulting from the policies of the liberal governments. More equal access to education across race, gender, and ethnicity, no matter how limited, can explain the reduction in wage inequality, particularly in the period 1970 to 2000 (Camps et al. 2007), and thus the reduction in overall income inequality.

Inequality, Education and Race

While the observed trend in the magnitude of educational inequality in the twentieth century generally has been pronounced, several scholars and educators have stressed the continued differences in school quality (Reimers 2006). Unequal educational facilities, including inadequate teacher skills provided to the non-white population has led to unequal chances in socioeconomic competition. According to proponents of the importance of differences in educational quality, the education system has been segmented and Native-Americans, blacks, mulattos, and mestizos have been placed in lower quality schools, with lower budgets and fewer resources, thus unable to provide for equality of education. While more prominent in the nineteenth century, the impact of differences in racial structure have led to continued differences in education and income levels. Table 2.2 presents measures of the extent to which access to education was unequal in the twentieth century. Children from parents in the lowest income deciles (normally non-whites) received only half/or fewer years of education then children from parents in the highest income decile.

Table 2.2 Average years of schooling according to income deciles, 1990s

Country	(1) Lowest income decile	(2) Highest income decile	(2)/(1) (%)
Argentina	7.1	14.24	2.0
Bolivia	6.44	12.12	1.88
Brazil	2.41	10.33	4.28
Colombia	4.86	6.68	1.37
Costa Rica	4.51	11.85	2.62
Chile	6.31	13.12	2.07
Ecuador	3.92	11.76	3.0
El Salvador	2.10	11.02	5.3
Honduras	2.73	8.98	3.28
Mexico	3.08	11.24	3.64
Peru	5.85	10.84	1.85
Uruguay	6.3	12.68	2.01
Venezuela	5.85	9.93	1.69

Data source Szekeley and Montes (2006)

From estimates of race diversity in Latin America (Rosenblat 1945) it appears that in 1825, before the mass migration from Europe to the Americas, Native Americans represented between 9.1% (Brazil) and 55.7% (Central America) of the total population. The information in regard to blacks is less complete, although Rosenblat (1945) estimates that there were about 387,000 blacks in continental Spanish America, plus 389,000 in Cuba and 260,000 in Guyana. Brazil's black population was 1960,000, equal to 16.4% the Brazilian population. The population of the black population enslaved in Latin America in 1825 was 75% of the total black population of about 3.4 million, meaning that Latin America had a larger proportion of free blacks that did the United States. This reflected, in part, the fact that after independence from Spain during the first decades of the nineteenth century slavery was abolished, although in Spanish America in several cases the process was gradual, not immediate, generally by a process called "the law of the free womb" (Engerman and Sokoloff 2012). In the country with the largest number of slaves as well as the largest share of slaves in the total population, Brazil, the ending of slavery was finally accomplished in 1888, seventeen years after the passage of the "Law of the Free Womb." Also note that, for the six countries listed by Rosenblat (see Table 2.1) the percentage of whites in the overall population in 1825 was generally less than 20%, while the white share in Brazilian population was 7.7%.

The picture seen in early nineteenth century changes significantly decades later with the development of mass migration from Europe. During this period about 60 million Europeans migrated to other countries of the world, particularly to North and South America, and to Australia (Hatton and Williamson 1998; Sanchez-Alonso 2007).[2] Most of those who migrated to South America came from southern Europe (Portugal, Spain, and Italy), with the preferred destinations of those from Spain being Argentina, Chile, and Uruguay, and, for Portugal, to Brazil. The second half of the nineteenth century saw marked changes in the racial structure of Latin America, as those nations receiving immigrants increased their share of whites in the population, raising the levels of education in these countries. Since the white European immigrants to Latin America tended to have more education than did the native-born whites at this time, this had served to raise education levels.

The liberal reforms of the twentieth century and the increased share of whites in the population both tended to increase educational levels as well as to reduce the extent of educational inequality. This helps to explain income and educational changes in Latin America over time. Bucciferro (2014) has stressed that in the case of Brazil racial differences were basic to understanding educational and income inequality, but although the situation improved during the last twenty years the gap remains wide. According to Engerman and Sokoloff (2012) and to Bucciferro (2014) racial equality in education has improved only in the recent past. In order to check this second set of hypotheses related to the impact of race on education and inequality we have performed several cross-sectional regressions based on the data sources already quoted in this paper. Data on ethnicity and race for the late twentieth century come from Alesina et al. (2003).

In Tables 2.3 and 2.4 we see evidence of the segmentation of the educational supply according to race. Only in 1960, however, we obtain statistically significant coefficients. But the sign and scope of

Table 2.3 The impact of race on years of schooling in 1960

Indian	0.0119	(0.01131)
White	0.0243***	(0.0067)
Black	−0.01443	(0.010a)
Constant	2.21295***	(0.39473)

$N = 19$; R^2=0.6430; (standard error in brackets); *$p < .1$, **$p < .05$, ***$p < .01$
Data sources Data on race from Rosenblat (1945) and data on education from Barro and Lee (2013)

Table 2.4 The impact of race on years of schooling in 2000

Indian	0.00822	(0.01978)
White	0.01984	(00.01175)
Black	−0.024748	(0.017721)
Constant	5.547209***	(0.69018)

$N = 19$; $R^2 = 0.3396$; (standard error in brackets); *$p < .1$, **$p < .05$, ***$p < .01$
Data sources Data on race from Alesina et al. (2003) and data on education from Barro and Lee (2013)

the coefficients are very similar for both dates. An increase of 1% in the proportion of whites in overall population has a significant effect in the years of schooling, of 0.0243 in 1960 and 0.01984 in 2000. A 1% increase in the proportion of blacks has a negative influence in the years of schooling in both years, while the results for the Indian population are positive but small. Therefore the regression results confirm that there are still wide differences in school attendance as late as end of the twentieth century. Whites remain in a privileged situation, enjoying more years of school than Native-Americans and blacks, the latter being most marginalized group (Tables 2.5 and 2.6).

Regarding the influence of race on educational inequality we find some evidence to support Bucciferro's (2014) hypothesis that between 1960 and 2000 there was a diminution of inequality according to race. The value of all coefficients diminish. The increase of Indian population by 2000 has a negative impact on educational inequality the same as in the case of whites, although in 2000 the size of the coefficient is higher and therefore the impact of the schooling of whites in educational

Table 2.5 The impact of race on educational inequality (educational gini) in 1960

Indian	0.1410	(0.2385)
White	−0.23628	(0.08325)
Black	0.36675*	(0.12548)
Constant	48.2922***	(4.29218)

$N = 20$; $R^2 = 0.6490$; (standard error in brackets); *$p < .1$, **$p < .05$, ***$p < .01$
Data sources Data on race from Rosenblat (1945) and data on educational gini from Clio Infra

Table 2.6 The impact of race on educational inequality (educational gini) in 2000

Indian	−0.02670	(0.06470)
White	−0.98174**	(0.03854)
Black	0.22328*	(0.05809)
Constant	28.9049***	(2.2289)

$N = 20$; $R^2 = 0.6777$; (standard error in brackets); *$p < .1$, **$p < .05$, ***$p < .01$
Data sources Data on race from Alesina et al. (2003) and data on educational gini from Clio Infra

inequality is greater than in the case of Indians. The impact of blacks in 2000 continues to be positive in increasing educational inequality even as the value of the coefficient diminishes. Educational inequalities diminished during the last decades of the twentieth century though blacks continued to be in a marginalized position and racial differences continued to be wide.

To describe the extent of education inequality by income level at the end of the twentieth century Table 2.2 (see also Table 2.7 [Parts I, II, III, IV]) compares the average number of years of schooling of those in the lowest decile of the income distribution with those in the highest decile in each country. In most of the countries for which we can obtain the necessary data, for most the period of education for the richest decile was at least double to that of the poorest decile. Among the poorest people, which contains a disproportionate number of Native-Americans and blacks, years of education varied from 2.1 to 7.1 years, while for the richest decile the range was from 6.7 to 14.24 years. Thus, while in the 1990s, most poor people did not succeed in completing primary schooling, a large number of those in the richest decile were able to come close to completing the secondary level. While the educational gaps among ethnic, racial, and income groups decreased in the twentieth century, the persistence of differentials help to maintain the differences in Latin American income inequality that, according to Deininger and Squire (1998), are, together with several African countries, the most unequal in the world.[3]

Table 2.7 Part I

Racial differences in education

(A)

Year	Country	Literacy rates	
		White	Colored
1860	Puerto Rico	19.8	2.1
1861	Cuba	38.5	5.3
1899	Cuba	51	28

Source Newland (1991) and Nelson (1950)

(B)

Year	Country	Literacy rates	
		Native White	Colored
1899	Cuba	46.7	28.0
1919	Cuba	62.7	53.1
1943	Cuba	72. (5	67.4

Source Nelson (1950)

Table 2.7 Part II

Adults. Percent by highest level of education, 1998									
	Mexico			Costa Rica			Chile		
	White	Moreno	Mul	White	Moreno	Mul	White	Moreno	Mul
Primary	22	36	53	50	54	54	35	38	50
Secondary	32	38	30	26	22	25	38	38	40
Higher	41	24	11	18	10	7	26	24	9

Source Reimers (2006)

Brazil	Whites ages 25–60: 7 years of schooling Black aged 25–60: 4 years of schooling
Guatemala	Indigenous: 2 years of schooling Non-indigenous: 5 years of schooling
Peru	Indigenous: less than 6 years of schooling Non-indigenous: >9 years of schooling
Bolivia	Indigenous: 4 years of schooling Non-indigenous: 9 years of schooling Indigenous 91% never in school, others 13%

Table 2.7 Part III

Race and level of education				
Brazil		1910	1920	1930
Literacy rate, population aged 6–10	White	55	62	67
		22	28	33
	Black	27	34	38
	Mixed	50	43	37
Never attended school	White	81	76	70
	Black	77	71	67
	Mixed	3.6	4.5	5.1
Completed elementary education	White	0.2	0.4	0.5
	Black	0.5	0.6	0.9
	Mixed	0.5	0.6	0.9

Source Musachio et al. (2014)

Percent illiterate (age 5+ older, males)	
Brazil in 2010	
White	Black
7.4	15.4

Percent highest Level of education			
Brazil in 1940			
	Elementary	Middle	Superior
White	71.4	18.7	10.0
Black	94.1	4.5	1.3
Mulatto	86.6	10.0	2.4

Source Vidal Luna and Klein (2014)

Literacy rate in percent	
Brazil in 1940	
White	52
Black	22
Mulatto	30

Source Luna and Klein (2014)

Table 2.7 Part IV

Illiteracy rate in the United States	Illiteracy rate in the United States	Illiteracy rate in the United States
Year	White	Black
1870	11.5	79.9
1900	6.2	44.5
1952	1.8	10.2
1979	0.4	1.6

College graduates (male)		
Year	Native-born White	Native-born Black
1940	6.8	1.5
1980	23.6	9.1
1997	30.1	16.3

Source Historical statistics

Conclusion

There have been major changes in the level of education achieved in Latin America, as well as some narrowing of racial and ethnic differences. Nevertheless, there remain significant differences in the amount and quality of education received by the non-white population relative to the white population. Moreover, despite the narrowing of differences in education, the disparities in income distribution persisted throughout the twentieth century. Clearly the continuity of political inequality from the settlement period has not been fully overcome, and even reforms in the education systems had not been able to overcome the other institutional factors that maintained inequality. While some changes have been shown to be possible to achieve more equality in levels of education, it will no doubt require other methods to close the present gaps. With the spread of education, a diminution of wage inequality during the last decades of the twentieth century has been observed (Camps 2009). It is possible that these same forces, more specifically the sharp diminution of educational inequality during the twentieth century and, thus far, in the twenty-first century, may explain the decrease of income inequality during the first decades of the twenty-first century as reported by several authors based on the study of household budgets (ECLAC 2012).

Notes

1. See also Engerman and Sokoloff (2012: 139). They point out that by 1914 Argentinean literacy rates were 59% among foreign-born and 40% among natives. Rates in Uruguay were very similar.
2. See also Maluquer de Motes et al. (1991–1994). This is a 12 volume set of monographs on Spanish emigration to Latin America.
3. Educational attainment differences in Latin American countries from 1960 to 2003 are also presented by Hanushek and Woessman (2012) which provide similar results.

Bibliography

Acemoglu, D., Johnson, S., Robinson, J.A., "The Colonial Origins of Comparative Development: An Empirical Investigation", *The American Economic Review*, 91, no. 5 (2011): 1369–1401.

Acemoglu, D., Robinson, J.A., "De Facto Political Power and Institutional Persistence", *American Economic Review*, 96, no. 2 (2006): 319–324.

Alesina, A., Easterly, W., Devleeschauwer, A., Kurlat, S., Wacziarg, R.T., "Fraccionalization", *Journal of Economic Growth*, VIII (2003): 155–194.

Allen, R.C., Murphy, T.E, Schneider, E.B., "Una de cal y otra de arena: Building Comparable Real Wages in Global Perspective", Revista de Historia Econmómica. *A Journal of Iberian and Latin American Economic History*, 33, no. 1 (2015): 61–75.

Arroyo-Abad, L., "Persistent Inequality? Trade, Factor Endowments, and Inequality in Republican Latin America", *Journal of Economic History*, 73, no. 1 (2013): 38–78.

Astorga, P., Bergés, A.R., Fitzgerald, E.V.K., "The Standard of Living in Latin America During the Twentieth Century", *Economic History Review*, 58, no. 4 (2005): 756–796.

Barro, R.J., Lee, J.-W., "A New Data Set of Educational Attainment in the World, 1950–2010", *Journal of Development Economics*, 104C (2013): 184–198.

Bertola, L., Castelnovo, C., Rodríguez, J., Willebald, H., "Between the Colonial Heritage and the First Globalization Boom: On Income Inequality in the Southern Cone", *Revista de Historia Económica. Journal of Iberian and Latin American Economic History*, 28, no. 2 (2010): 307–341.

Bertola, L., Ocampo, J.A., *El desarrollo económica de América Latina desde la Independencia*. México, Fondo de Cultura Económica, 2013.

Bucciferro, J.R., "Race and Brazilian Inequality in the Long Run", Paper presented at the Conference: Latin American Inequality in the Long Run, Buenos Aires (2014), http://sites.middlebury.edu/ehrgc/files/2015/04/Bucciferro.pdf.

Camps, E., Camou, M., Maubrigades, S., Mora-Sitja, N., "Globalization and Wage Inequality in South and East Asia and Latin America: A Gender Approach", Ideas RePec Publishing Web (2007), https://ideas.repec.org/p/upf/upfgen/970.html.

Camps, E., "Globalization and Culture Shaping the Gender Gap: A Comparative Analysis of Urban Latin America and East Asia (1970–2000)", Ideas RePec Publishing Web (2009), https://ideas.repec.org/p/upf/upfgen/1145.html.

Coatsworth, J.H., "Inequality, Institutions and Economic Growth in Latin America", *Journal of Latin American Studies*, 40, no. 3 (2008): 545–569.

Deininger, K., Squire, L., "New Ways of Looking at Old Issues: Inequality and Growth", *Journal of Development Economics*, 57, no. 2 (1998): 259–288.

ECLAC, *Structural Change for Equality: An Integrated Approach to Development*. Santiago de Chile, 2012.

Engerman, S.L., Sokoloff, K.L., *Economic Development in the Americas Since 1500: Endowments and Institutions*. New York, Cambridge University Press and NBER, 2012.

Fitzgerald, V.F.K., "Economic Development and Fluctuations in Earnings Inequality in the Very Long Run: The Evidence from Latin America, 1900–2000", *Journal of International Development*, 20 (2008): 1028–1048.

Frankema, E., *Has Latin America Always Been Unequal? A Comparative Study of Asset and Income Inequality in the Long Twentieth Century*. Leiden, Koninklijke, 2009.

Goldin, C., Katz, L., *The Race Between Education and Technology*. Cambridge, MA, Harvard University Press, 2008.

Hanushek, E.A., Woessman, L., "Schooling, Educational Achievement and the Latin American Growth Puzzle", *Journal of Development Economics*, 99 (2012): 497–512.

Hatton, T., Williamson, J.G., *The Age of Mass Migration: Causes and Economic Impact*. New York, Oxford University Press, 1998.

Landes, D., *The Wealth and Poverty of Nations: Why Some Are Rich and Some so Poor*. New York, W. W. Norton, 1998.

Lindert, P., "The Unequal Lag in Latin American Schooling Since 1900: Follow the Money", *Revista de Historia Económica. A Journal of Iberian and Latin American Economic History*, 28, no. 2 (2010): 375–405.

Maddison, A., *The World Economy: Historical Statistics*. Paris, OECD, 2003.

Maluquer de Motes, J., Nadal, J., Macías, A., *Cruzar el Charco*. Spain and Colombres: Fundación Archivo de Indianos, 12 vols., 1991–1994.

Musachio, A., Martinez Fritscher, A., Viarengo, M., "Colonial Institutions, Trade Shocks, and the Diffusion of Elementary Education in Brazil, 1889–1930", *Journal of Economic History*, 74, no. 3 (2014): 730–766.

Nelson, L., *Rural Cuba*. Minneapolis, University of Minnesota Press, 1950.

Newland, C., "La educación elemental en Hispanoamérica: desde la independencia hasta la centralización de los sistemas educativos nacionales", *Hispanic American Historical Review*, 71 no. 2 (1991): 335–364.

Prados de la Escosura, L., "Inequality and Poverty in Latin America: A Long-Run Exploration", in *The New Comparative Economic History*, edited by T.J. Hatton, K. O'Rourke, A.M. Taylor. Cambridge, MA, MIT Press, 2007, pp. 291–315.

Reimers, F., "Education and Social Progress", in *The Cambridge Economic History of Latin America*, edited by V. Blumer-Thomas, J. Coatsworth, R. Cortés Conde, vol. II, *The Long Twentieth Century*. New York, Cambridge University Press, 2006, pp. 427–480.

Rosenblat, A., *La población indígena de América desde 1492 hasta la actualidad*. Buenos Aires, Instituto de Filología de Buenos Aires, 1945.

Sanchez-Alonso, Blanca, "The Other Europeans: Immigration into Latin America and the International Labour Market, (1870–1930)", *Revista de Historia Económica. Journal of Iberian and Latin American Economic History*, 15, no. 3 (2007): 395–426.

Székeley, M., Montes, A., "Poverty and Inequality", in *The Cambridge Economic History of Latin America*, edited by V. Blumer Thomas, J. Coatsworth, R. Cortes Conde, vol. II, *The Long Twentieth Century*. New York, Cambridge University Press, 2006, pp. 585–646.

Vidal Luna, F., Klein, H.S., *The Economic and Social History of Brazil Since 1899*. New York, Cambridge University Press, 2014.

Williamson, J.G., "Five Centuries of Latin American Inequality", *Revista de Historia Económica. Journal of Iberian and Latin American Economic History*, 28, no. 2 (2010): 227–252.

Williamson, J.G., "Latin American Inequality: Colonial Origins, Commodity Booms, or a Missed 20th Century Leveling?" NBER Working Paper No. 20915, Cambridge, MA, 2015.

3

Education and Inequality in North America in the Long Term with Special Reference to the United States

Abstract Trends in inequality and education in the United States are well known thanks to the research and publications by Goldin and Katz (*The Race Between Education and Technology*. Harvard University Press, Cambridge, 2008) and Lindert and Williamson (*Unequal Gains: American Growth and Inequality Since 1700*. Princeton University Press, Princeton and Oxford, 2016) among others. Since the last third of the nineteenth century, and even before (Engerman and Sokoloff in *Economic Development in the Americas Since 1500: Endowments and Institutions*. Cambridge University Press and NBER, New York, 2012) decentralized institutions at the local and county level and latter the States supplied public education starting with primary education and evolving to secondary and College education. Education was skill biased but supply grew at the same path than demand till the last third of the century. After the 1970s demand was higher than supply leading to the increase of inequality. Rightward political shifts, acceleration in the adoption of labor saving technologies, the massive rise in labor-intensive imports from emerging nations born by the second era of globalization

E. Camps-Cura, *Changes in Population, Inequality and Human Capital Formation in the Americas in the Nineteenth and Twentieth Centuries*, Palgrave Studies in Economic History,
https://doi.org/10.1007/978-3-030-21351-0_3

and the explosion of financial activity after six decades of tighter regulation are all factors that also help to explain this last rise of inequality according to Lindert and Williamson.

Keywords North America · Public education · Skill biased · Globalization · Inequality

During the twenty-first century there has been a growing interest in the study of inequality of world citizens. From the initial use of Gini coefficients (Bourguignon and Morrison 2002) the main improvement has been to use Theil indexes that allow to decompose inequality in across countries inequality and inside a country inequality (Sala i Martin 2006) and recently the stress to study of inside a country inequality has increased. In this respect the study of the United States is especially relevant since by the end of the twentieth century this nation was the most unequal country among rich ones (poorest countries from Latin America and Africa reach highest levels).

When looking at the reasons behind inequality, research on the productivity evolution, education, and globalization trends become especially relevant.

While in the United States inequality levels were pretty high during the last third of the nineteenth century, they had a decreasing trend from 1900 to 1975 and again and upward trend from 1975 to 2019 (Goldin and Katz 2008; Lindert and Williamson 2016). Trends during the first globalization era are some of the aspects that help to explain the rise of inequality during the late nineteenth century and beginnings of the twentieth century (Hatton and Williamson 1998). This was the era of mass migration from overpopulated Europe to other continents such as the Americas with lower population density. The massive arrival of population implied a substantial increase of the labor supply and therefore a downward pressure on real wages. On the other hand more population demanded more capital and land and therefore rents and profits surged. The wage/rental ratio decreased implying higher levels of inequality. According to Lindert and Williamson (2016) the Kuznet's inverse U of the distribution of income applied to the United States from 1860 to 1970. Inequality increased from 1860 up to the first third of the twentieth century and was followed by the Greatest Leveling of all times during the Golden Age of Capitalism.

Goldin and Katz (2008) have stressed that the twentieth century was the human capital century and therefore the American century. During most of the period, levels of education were higher in the United States with respect to other rich countries. This trend already began in the nineteenth century when a network of public schools was created by local or county authorities. Levels of literacy of the white population were already high in a sample of selected counties and towns by the mid of the nineteenth century (Engerman and Sokoloff 2012). In addition these schools were open, forgiving and gender neutral. According to Goldin and Katz this educational superiority had a role on technological evolution and economic growth. More education meant more capabilities to innovate and creating new machines. Economic growth requires educated workers, managers, entrepreneurs. In spite of the fact that initially the United States did not lead some of the branches of the second industrial revolution such as chemicals, it soon became the leader in the production of automobiles, such as Ford, that in turn made a revolution in the organization for the firm. Big firms were created and the organization of labor was also transformed (fordism, taylorism)—see Chandler (1977). According to Goldin and Katz (2008) more education allowed for more technological change and therefore more economic growth. Since the last third of the nineteenth century education was skill biased and dependent on the technologies of the time. During the second industrial revolution of the late nineteenth century workers had a non competing human capital, since most of them only had education at the primary levels. In this period, and in spite of the general trend of real wages to increase, workers at the basis of the production process undertaking very simple tasks, had lower education and lower wages, which helps to explain why inequality still remained high in spite of the initial spread of education.

During most of the twentieth century a new pressure to create more secondary schools and latter college studies universalized education in high schools, technical schools, and to a less extent universities. This pressure was not from the top to the bottom from a large part of the citizens to the government. It was a demand by most of the population. Generally speaking parents wanted that the education of their children was better than that of their own. This fact is illustrated by Goldin and Katz giving details on a lot of citizens movements and demonstrations.

Literacy and numeracy allowed the population to sign contracts, to vote, to understand the instructions in manuals to deal with new machines. This is why the American century was the human capital century. On the other hand as already stated the educational system was less elite than in Europe. Economic growth took place because a greater level of education has as a result in higher levels of labor productivity. But according to Goldin and Katz, and in spite education is a necessary condition for economic growth, other variables are also crucial. Otherwise the problems of underdevelopment would have been solved since time ago. A democratic, not corrupted and representative government is also another condition for economic growth the same as the security of property rights (social capital). And these conditions were highly developed in North America where, for instance property rights of innovation, patents, were more developed than in Europe since the starting point.

Technological change and economic growth had as a consequence the increase of the demand of educated workers and this fact could have as a result an increase in inequality among other consequences. But during the first three quarters of the twentieth century the trend was long term economic growth and declining inequality. This trend can be explained because the increase in the demand of educated labor came together with the increase of the supply. As an average, in the years 1870–1950 every decade involved an increase of the educational supply of 0.8 years and this process accelerated during the Golden Age of Capitalism. Educational advance, being skill biased, could cause more inequality since workers at the top of the income hierarchy may receive more education than those at the bottom. But till the 1970s education demand at all levels of skill increased at the same path than supply shaping a trend toward a more equal distribution of income. This is when the Leontief paradox applied to the United States. In spite of the fact that the United States was the country with more physical capital of the world, the value of its exports contained more labor than capital than the value of its imports, because the United States was not only the country with more physical capital of the world but also the country with more human capital (Camps 2013).

Educational attainment was rapid till 1975 but educational advance slowed considerably afterwards. This slowdown particularly affected race and ethnic minorities but was gender neutral. Indeed gender differences narrowed (Lindert and Williamson 2016). This was not caused by new technologies and the spread of personal computers. This came together with a productivity change that slowed since 1975 and only recovered after 1990, not soon enough. But labor force expanded more rapidly than did population and therefore the decrease in productivity was higher than the decrease of income per head. Levels of inequality rose again after 1975 and inequality at the beginnings of the twenty-first century was as high as during the great depression. The reasons behind this new increase of inequality, according to Goldin and Katz (2008) are that while educational demand continued to increase, educational supply slowed for the overall labor force by early 1980s. An important part of the American Dream till then, that children would be better off than their parents was threatened. The nations of Europe and Asia followed America's lead and some, in recent years have begun to exceed US high school and college graduation rates and intellectual results. Even if in economic terms the United States continues to be the leader, European and some Asian nations are converging (Europe and Japan since the start of 1970s). And the slower path of growth of education supply with respect to demand has caused a new surge of inequality, a problem of major concern among US citizens. This has come together with the reform of the educational system which has meant the creation of Vouchers, Charter Schools, public funding for church-based schools which consequences that only will be visible in the forthcoming future. Not only the quantity of education is lagging behind but also its quality. According to Goldin and Katz, among the younger cohorts, the United States lags behind Europe and Japan, the previous followers, in the results in exams on reading, maths, science.

According to Lindert and Williamson (2016) the sharp increase of inequality from 1970s to 2010 can be explained by the educational and labor force variables developed by Goldin and Katz but they add other variables (rightward political shifts, acceleration in the adoption of labor saving technologies, the explosion of financial activity after six decades of tighter regulation…) and in spite all of them had an impact on the increase of levels of inequality in this chapter we want to specially outline the effects of the second globalization era.

The second era of globalization was less intensive than the first international migration flows, and more intensive in the growth of capital movements and trade. International migration movements only attained and intensity equivalent of a half of the one achieved during the first globalization era and were South to North, therefore from poor to rich countries (increasing the supply of unskilled labor in developed countries). This was also the case in North America, where, and in spite of the regulation of migration movements, the origins of migration were in the south, mostly Mexico and other countries of South America. This makes a big difference with regard to the first era of globalization when we have seen the movement was mostly from overpopulated Europe to other less populated countries such as the Americas. In this respect we'll see that European overpopulation, caused by the demographic transition of the nineteenth century represents an exception in the world context. In the rest of the world population explosion caused by the demographic transition took place during the twentieth century.

We therefore can remark that population movements, increasing the supply of unskilled labor force as well as we'll see now trade, were all causing the increase on inequality. Regarding trade we want to stress here the massive rise of labor-intensive imports from emerging nations, particularly China and India since the 1980s and 1990s. These are the most populated countries in the world. By the beginnings of the twenty-first century China had a population of 1300 million and India 1200 million, and the two nations together accounted for around 40% of the world population (7000 million). In the case of China this country began to grow and to catch up after the death of the communist leader Mao Tse Tung and the start of a progressive process of economic liberalization. China (and also India) because of their abundant labor force had a cheap labor supply. With the beginnings of economic liberalization they began to industrialize on the bases as we said of abundant and cheap labor which gave comparative advantage to export (Sala i Martin 2006). At the starting point exports were addressed to Asian countries but soon reached the industrialized world, also North America. In the case of the United States the cheap imports of manufactures from East and South Asia was another engine increasing inequality (Lindert and Williamson 2016). Therefore, this trend in trade movements together with movements of labor all of them had as an effect the increase of inequality during the second era of globalization.

Summarizing a lot of education and institutional features of North America (human capital and social capital) caused a substantial decrease of income inequality in the period from 1900 to 1970s. From 1970s to 2010, together with the second globalization era and changes in international trade, labor markets and human capital formation, all of them caused a new trend of inequality evolution. Inequality began to increase again, at the same path that during the first era of globalization and by now the United States are the most unequal nation of the developed world.

The Summary of the Empirical Evidence

Data Sources and Methodology

In order to finish this chapter, we want to present the long run trends of the evolution of human capital, real wages, and GDP per capita both in the United States and Canada by means of their time series evolution. Data on human capital include education (years of schooling) and health (life expectancies) De data sources for education in the United States are CPS Historical Time Series Tables, United States, Census Bureau, and Clio Infra in the case of Canada. Data sources for life expectancies are the Historical Statistics of the United States Millenial Edition Online for the United States, and WHO for Canada. Data on real wages com form Clio Infra, in both cases, the United States and Canada. And data on GDP per capita are from the Maddison project also in both cases the United States and Canada.

The Time Series on Human Capital, Real Wages, and GDP Per Capita During the Twentieth Century

In Figs. 3.1, 3.2, 3.3, and 3.4, we present the relevant variables on the evolution of the already mentioned time series. Real wages evolution has been used as an estimation of labor productivity evolution. In Fig. 3.1 on the United States we can see that real wages and therefore labor productivity surged at a quick path from 1925 to 1975 and afterwards stagnated from 1975 to 2000. This result is in line with results presented before in this chapter, of stagnation of labor productivity and increase of levels of inequality after 1975.

Contemporaneously human capital decelerated its rhythm of growth. The trend toward a stagnation of labor productivity is nonetheless not visible in the evolution of GDP per capita (income per capita) since total population grew less than the labor force, in line with conclusions by Goldin and Katz.

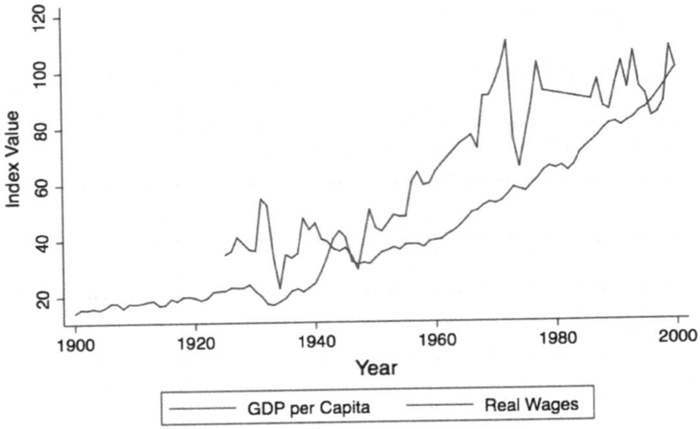

Fig. 3.1 GDP per capita and real wages in the US, 1900–2000

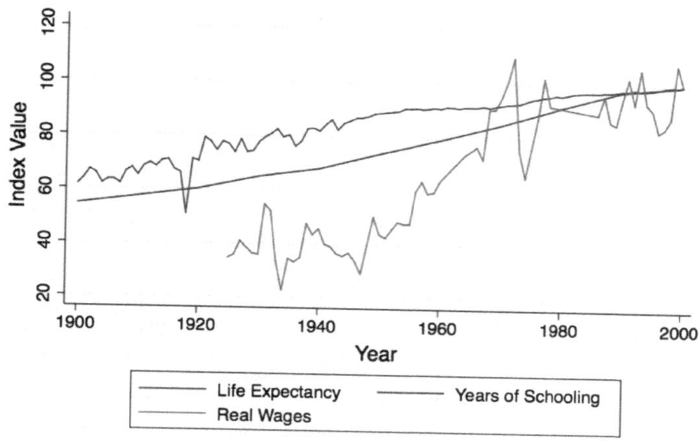

Fig. 3.2 Life expectancy, years of schooling and real wages in the US, 1900–2000

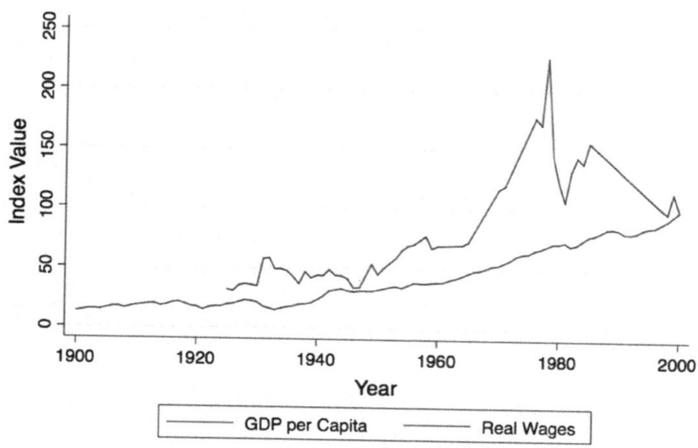

Fig. 3.3 GDP per capita and real wages in Canada, 1900–2000

The trends of growth in Canada are more modest but square well with results on the United States, even if the global trends of growth of labor productivity (real wages) and GDP per capita are lower. In fact, the terms human capital century and the American century refer mostly to the United States.

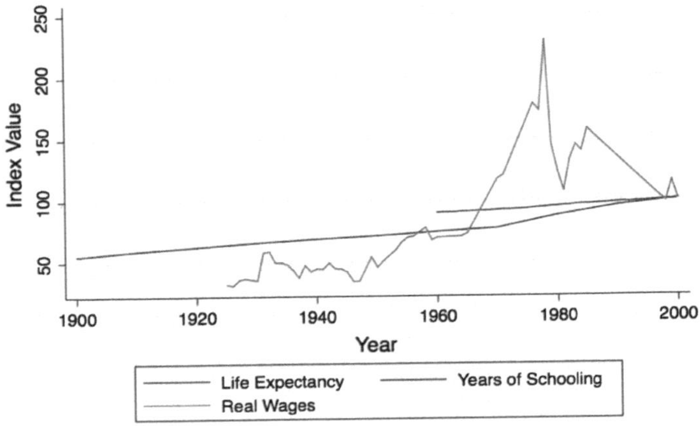

Fig. 3.4 Life expectancy, years of schooling and real wages in Canada, 1900–2000

Bibliography

Bourguignon, F., Morrison, J., "Inequality Among World Citizens, 1820–1992", *American Economic Review*, September 2002, 7272–7344.

Camps, E., *Historia económica mundial. La formación de4 la economía internacional*. Madrid, McGraw-Hill, 2013.

Chandler, A., *The Visible Hand: The Managerial Revolution in American Business*. Cambridge, MA, Harvard University Press, 1977.

Engerman, S.L., Sokoloff, K.L., *Economic Development in the Americas Since 1500: Endowments and Institutions*. New York, Cambridge University Press and NBER, 2012.

Goldin, C., Katz, L., *The Race Between Education and Technology*. Cambridge, MA, Harvard University Press, 2008.

Hatton, T., Williamson, J.G., *The Age of Mass Migration: Causes and Economic Impact*. New York, Oxford University Press, 1998.

Lindert, P.H., Williamson, J.G., *Unequal Gains: American Growth and Inequality Since 1700*. Princeton and Oxford, Princeton University Press, 2016.

Sala i Martin, X., "The World Distribution of Income: Falling Poverty and Convergence Period", *Quarterly Journal of Economics*, 121, no. 2, May 2006.

4

World Population Growth and Fertility Patterns, 1960–2010: A Simple Model Explaining the Evolution of the World's Fertility—The Americas in a Comparative Framework

Abstract In this paper we attempt to describe the general reasons behind the world population explosion in the twentieth century. The size of the population at the end of the century in question, deemed excessive by some, was a consequence of a dramatic improvement in life expectancies, attributable, in turn, to scientific innovation, the circulation of information, and economic growth. Nevertheless, fertility is a variable that plays a crucial role in differences in demographic growth. We identify infant mortality, female education levels, and racial identity as important exogenous variables affecting fertility. It is estimated that in poor countries one additional year' of primary schooling for women leads to 0.614 childless per couple on average (worldwide). While it may be possible to identify a global tendency towards convergence in demographic trends, particular attention should be paid to the case of Africa, not only due to its different demographic patterns, but also because much of the continent's population has yet to experience improvement in quality of life generally enjoyed across the rest of the planet.

E. Camps-Cura, *Changes in Population, Inequality and Human Capital Formation in the Americas in the Nineteenth and Twentieth Centuries*, Palgrave Studies in Economic History,
https://doi.org/10.1007/978-3-030-21351-0_4

Keywords Population growth · Life expectancies · Fertility · Scientific innovation · Demographic transition

Introduction

Today, most of the policymakers and people who deal with social, economic, and demographic issues regard population growth as a problem. That notion, of course, dates back at least to Malthus and his predictions based on the dynamics of the population growth, vis-a-vis resource availability. In the early twenty-first century, prices of certain basic food products have begun to rise. It is widely felt that if there are too many people now, the situation will be even more difficult in the future. Although the prices of calories and energy have risen over the last decade, the world is not only increasingly populated but also increasingly industrialized and rich. The question of whether or not there are too many people deserves more attention since population growth can have pros and cons. In the nineteenth and twentieth centuries, population growth and increased population density were considered an asset for many nations as factors contributing to: economies of scale and cheaper labor, and the bases for urbanization and economic growth.

Despite all the concerns, the population, while still growing, has been doing so at diminishing rates since 1970. A key question is whether there are too many children, with population growth reflecting a high rate of fertility, or whether the population explosion in recent years has been due to improved health standards and reduction of mortality, stemming from material prosperity and technological progress.

In this paper, we aim to provide preliminary data that may help paint a picture of the variables that influence demographic growth worldwide and their regional variance. The intention in this exploratory article is to set out some working hypothesis on the reasons behind demographic growth and its most plausible future evolution. In forthcoming papers, we hope to draw on preliminary results to model the worldwide population dynamics for the second half of the twentieth century, based on economic, demographic, and cultural factors, including, in particular, female and child education, and employment, infant mortality, and changing income levels, in addition to ethnic differentials. We shall first concentrate on the issue of whether the determining variable behind demographic growth is fertility (and therefore reproductive habits) or mortality (and therefore progress in the health arena). We will refrain from analyzing nuptiality here, since religion has ceased to be as important in terms of fertility dynamics in the period under consideration, having lost much of the influence that, before 1960, it had held over family formation and the age at which couples conceived their first child.

Furthermore, finding a homogeneous indicator for family formation and nuptiality for historical populations would be very difficult. Most of the literature, including the majority of papers on historical demography, deal with Europe and the United States, populations that were part of the "European demographic system", in which children were conceived by married, monogamous couples (indeed, most statistical calculations on nuptiality and fertility are based on this sort of family arrangement). That was certainly the case in Western Europe, where, as Voth and Voigtländer (2013) have demonstrated, delaying the age of marriage reduced fertility by a third. That created a situation of low demographic pressure on economic assets, leading to a marginal surplus of income and increase in consumption which economic vibrancy of preindustrial western Europe can be attributed. When extending the sample to all the world's civilizations and religions, however, it is necessary to make certain simplifications regarding the culture of, and motives for, marrying and having children. Polygamy is a feature of some African societies where the ability to conceive children basically depends on women's fertility rather than other social or cultural determinants, such as those applicable in most western societies. We seek to stress our awareness of this limitation, and of the fact that attempting to capture fertility patterns that are common to and statistically significant for all the world's people entails a loss of explanatory power. The questions we search to answer on the basis of the data and the results which follow this introduction are only relevant to fertility patterns in the second half of the twentieth century. We think that the limitations of nuptiality involved in the nineteenth-century European demographic system would be relevant if fertility were increasing and the number of years in which women can conceive were a key factor in fertility levels. As will become apparent, our intention is not to explain which factors are obstacles to female fertility reaching its full potential, but rather to explain the main factors behind declining fertility. Social factors preventing the maximum reproductive level being attained are thus of secondary importance.

Are Demographic Patterns Converging Across the World?

In the concluding volume of the seminal work on the demographic transition in Europe (Coale and Watkins 1986), it is stated that despite there being sharp contrasts in the economic achievements of the continent's countries, the demographic transition took place at much the same time inside most of Western Europe. It appears that once a threshold level of per capita GDP was crossed in nineteenth-century Europe, epidemics and famines ceased to threaten the population, and adult and infant mortality diminished. More recently, as Becker et al. (2005) indicate life expectancy has converged across nations over the last half century.

The timing of declines in mortality throughout the world has thus been more similar than would be predicted on the basis of economic factors. Meanwhile, urbanization and industrial growth brought about a reduction in legitimate fertility. As a result of the circulation of information due to internal migrations, the communications revolution and rising levels of literacy, the influence of towns and cities on the demographic behavior of extended regions and countries increased (Wrigley 2004; De Vries 1985; Voth and Voigtländer 2013). That is why, despite economic divergence, population dynamics tended to converge. The scope that the transport revolution and migration offered for exchanging information on improving health and reproductive practices was one of the factors that fostered territorial homogeneity and alignment of demographic variables, not only in nineteenth-century England but also Europe in general. Certain authors have used micro historical methods to emphasize the distinctive features of several European regions, highlighting religious beliefs and socioeconomic variables that may help to explain why behavior in different regions is similar but not always identical (Brown and Guinnane 2002).

The European demographic transition is unique in that it took place relatively early. According to World Bank datasets and Annual Reports, most of the world still had high rates both of fertility and of infant mortality in 1960. Thus, in the post-WWII period, the countries benefiting from the Golden Age of Capitalism had not yet experienced the demographic transition. That is particularly true of poor countries, those affected by the tropical pattern of poverty. As late as 1995, those tropical countries were among the poorest in the world, a situation that has generated a long literature on the geographical reasons for economic growth or its absence. That, however, is not our main focus of interest here. The important consideration for our purposes is that in 1960, the poorest countries in the world (countries in the tropics) were those with the highest fertility and infant mortality rates, as well as the lowest rates of female and child education. It is plausible to think that the communications and information exchange network referred to earlier had still to develop in the countries in question to pave the way for declines in fertility and infant mortality, mirroring innovations already underway in the developed world.

The global scenario had changed significantly by 2010, however. By then, a time marked by the communications revolution, most of the world had shifted to modern demographic patterns. Thus, on the eve of the twenty-first century, much of the planet had undergone transition from high to relatively low fertility (and high to low infant mortality rates) the main exception being the countries of Sub-Saharan Africa. This is a striking case, as Sub-Saharan Africa is not only a high fertility region but also the region with the highest levels of infant and adult mortality. Thus, in this belated global demographic transition there is still a group of countries lagging behind, marked by characteristics that seem to limit economic growth. In Africa, this has meant international as well as civil wars, but also hunger and disease (pandemics) leading to death. Those factors help explain the high levels of mortality, as well as the high levels of fertility observed, bearing in mind the considerable probability of death during the first year of life.

Figures 4.1 and 4.2 and Tables 4.1a, 4.1b, 4.2a, 4.2b, and 4.3 show aspects of the world's demographic development by region. The tendency towards regional convergence of both fertility and infant mortality variables should be noted in the tables and figures. With some delay, the world's slowest-developing regions, demographically speaking, such as sub-Saharan Africa and South Asia, show a trend of convergence with the core countries of Europe and North America. To answer the question proposed above, that of why the world's population is growing, this growth is due not to an increase in fertility levels but to improved health conditions in a major group of countries. Adult and infant mortality rates have improved in all countries, with most of the world's population living longer and enjoying relatively higher living standards.

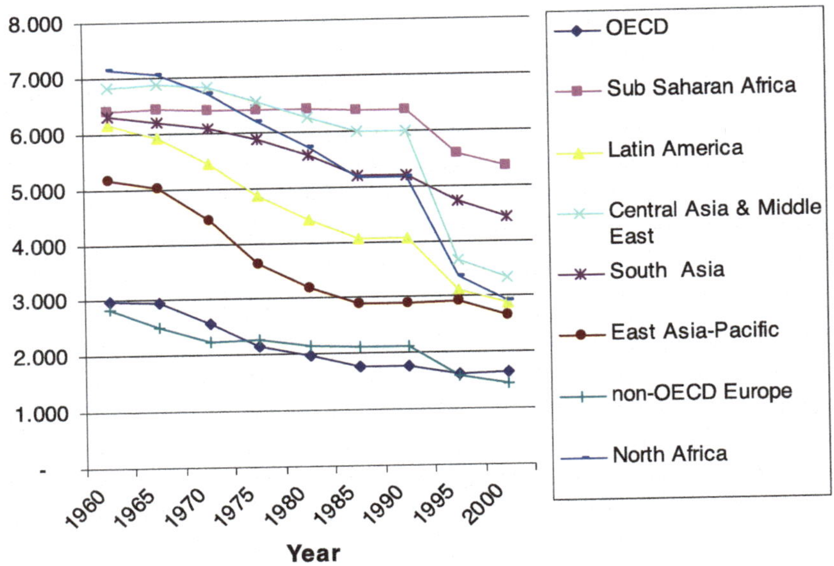

Fig. 4.1 Fertility rates in the world regions, 1960–2000 (*Source* World Bank datasets)

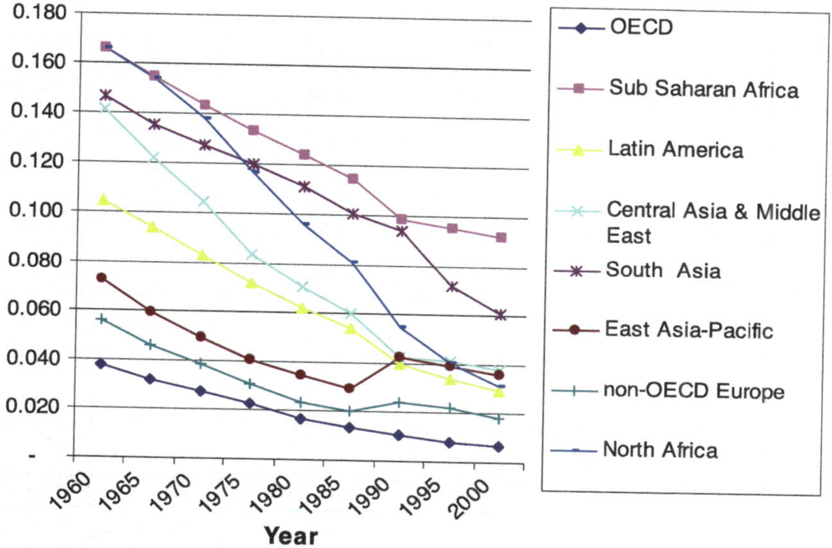

Fig. 4.2 Infant mortality rates in the world regions, 1960–2000 (*Source* World Bank datasets)

Table 4.1a Mean fertility by region, 1960 (births/women at reproductive age)

Fertility 1960	Mean	Std. Dev.	Min	Max
OECD	2.99	0.93	2.17	6.28
Sub Saharan Africa	6.41	0.82	4.06	8
Latin America	6.17	1.22	2.87	7.35
Central Asia and Middle East	6.82	1.22	3.87	7.75
South Asia	6.31	0.75	5.27	6.98
East Asia-Pacific	5.18	1.52	2.04	6.97
Non-OECD Europe	2.82	0.59	2.02	3.44
North Africa	7.16	0.13	7.03	7.34

Table 4.1b Mean fertility by region, 2010

Fertility, 2010	Mean	Std. Dev.	Min	Max
OECD	1.74	0.38	1.23	3.03
Sub Saharan Africa	4.62	1.22	1.47	7.06
Latin America	2.63	0.58	1.47	3.98
Central Asia and Middle East	3.98	0.80	1.67	4.70
South Asia	2.97	1.42	1.75	6.29
East Asia-Pacific	2.76	1.17	1.13	5.58
Non-OECD Europe	1.43	0.13	1.15	1.56
North Africa	2.98	1.03	2.13	5.2

Source World Bank datasets

Table 4.2a Mean infant mortality rates by region, 1960 (deaths of children younger than one/births)

IMR, 1960	Mean	Std. Dev.	Min	Max
OECD	0.04	0.04	0.003	0.18
Sub Saharan Africa	0.17	0.03	0.068	0.219
Latin America	0.10	0.04	0.05	0.19
Central Asia and Middle East	0.14	0.05	0.031	0.212
South Asia	0.15	0.05	0.069	0.186
East Asia-Pacific	0.07	0.05	0.02	0.163
Non-OECD Europe	0.06	0.02	0.03	0.088
North Africa	0.17	0.01	0.158	0.178

Table 4.2b Mean infant mortality rates by region, 2010

IMR, 2010	Mean	Std. Dev.	Min	Max
OECD	0.004	0.003	0.003	0.003
Sub Saharan Africa	0.07	0.03	0.01	0.12
Latin America	0.02	0.01	0.005	0.07
Central Asia and Middle East	0.02	0.016	0.006	0.05
South Asia	0.04	0.02	0.01	0.074
East Asia-Pacific	0.02	0.01	0.002	0.05
Non-OECD Europe	0.01	0.004	0.003	0.019
North Africa	0.03	0.022	0.013	0.07

Table 4.3 Mortality and Race; twentieth century US

	Evolution of life expectancies at birth (male)		
	White	Black	Difference (absolute) (years)
1900	48	33	15
1920	56	47	9
1940	63	52	11
1960	68	60	8
1990	73	64	9
1998	74	67	7

Evolution of infant mortality rates (deaths during the first year of life/ births)*1000			
	White	Black	Difference
1915	98.6	181.2	82.6
1930	60.1	99.5	39.4
1940	43.2	72.9	29.7
1960	22.9	44.3	21.4
1980	10.9	22.2	11.3
1998	6.0	14.3	8.3

Source Carter et al., Historical Statistics of the United States, Volume 1

A Simple Model of the Reasons for Declining Fertility

The most relevant studies (and the data we present here) indicate a tendency towards convergence across nations in fertility and mortality in the period under consideration. We have also observed that the relationship between demographic variables and income levels is non-linear. As mentioned previously, life expectancies improved considerably in the twentieth century, most notably up the 1960s, thanks to improvements in nutrition and health (Fogel 2004). Generally speaking, life expectancies appear to have diminishing returns in relation to income, and Fogel predicts that they will not increase by more than 10–15 years during the twenty-first century (compared to having almost doubled in the twentieth century). In section "A Simple Model of the Reasons for Declining Fertility" we indicated that fertility has tended to converge at a historically low level, close to replacement level. Africa is still the continent with the highest fertility rates. High fertility in poor countries mainly in sub-Saharan Africa remains a matter of concern for the UN. Even if fertility rates are diminishing, present demographic patterns and Net Reproduction Rates point to the population of the group of countries in question doubling every 30 years. If all the world's countries, including those of sub-Saharan Africa, achieve fertility rates close to the replacement level, by 2050 the world population should peak at 9.1 billion, a level most economic authorities hope will not be exceeded (Sachs 2008, p. 167). In this period there will be a dramatic shift in the regional distribution of the global population. Since below-replacement fertility in the developed nations has already begun, and it should take several decades for this to occur in the less developed world, the share of the developed nations in world population will decline.

The common view of demographic planners is that we should try to achieve fertility levels close to or below the replacement level, not to have population increase. In this section we model the factors that influence fertility and in the next we present a regression analysis based on the variables included in the model discussed here.

In Fig. 4.3 we divide the variables that affect fertility into endogenous and exogenous variables. The endogenous variables are those related to economic growth, which constitute the main set of variables

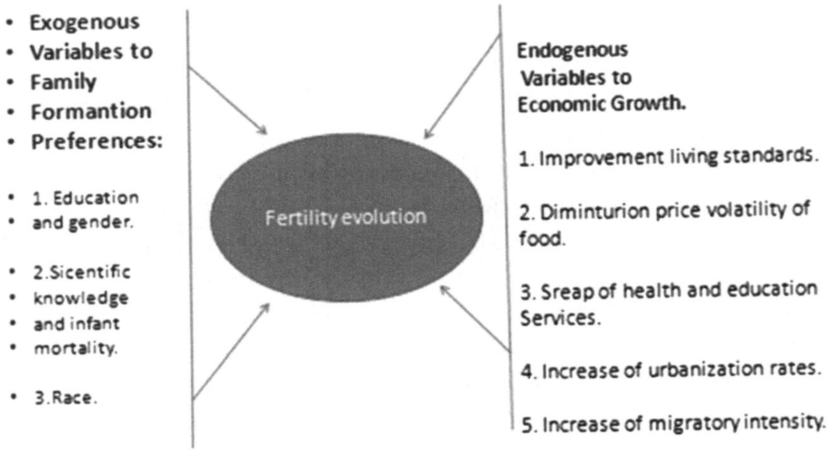

Fig. 4.3 A model on the variables affecting fertility

considered by most of the models that deal with the European demographic transition referred to in section "A Simple Model of the Reasons for Declining Fertility". Also in, we made the point that in most studies of fertility of the continent, fertility rate reductions are generally linked to endogenous factors associated with economic growth, such as: improved living standards, urbanization and internal migrations, an improved supply of health, increased education, improved agricultural technologies, and changes in food prices. The first variable we consider is the impact on fertility of changes in the level of per capita GDP.

Clearly, exogenous variables not directly related to economic growth can also explain fertility in poor countries in the decades under consideration. They include: infant mortality, female education, and factors related to racial diversity. According to Williamson (2001) infant mortality has played a major role in explaining fertility changes in countries in East and South Asia in recent decades. He regards this variable as exogenous since it mainly depends on scientific knowledge (vaccines, antibiotics, penicillin, etc.) developed through medical innovation in the West in the twentieth century, as well as successful public health interventions. Due to a substantial increase in the number of children surviving their first year of life, the reduction in infant mortality led to a fall in total number of births per family, due to longer child spacing as a result of prolonged lactation. Also parents reduced the number of children to ensure the continued survival of their existing offspring, as well as the ability, when desired, to achieve a certain number of live children with fewer births.

Another exogenous factor influencing families' preferences in terms of having more or less children consists of education levels for the mothers. According to data provided by Barro and Lee (2013) on the female/male education ratio (calculated on the basis of the number of years people spend in the education system by regions), the amount of education women receive is influenced by culture, and the regions with lowest fertility (and education) levels are in East and South Asia (see Boserup 1970; Barro and Lee 2000; Sen 1990, 1992, 2003).

However, in societies where families do invest in human capital, the result can be an increase in the value of women's paid work (wages), affecting the opportunity costs involved in unpaid domestic work, including the bearing and raising of children. Women's preferences consequently change and they begin to allocate more time to paid work and less to reproductive work and other unpaid activities, ultimately causing a fall in fertility and a rise in female labor force participation (Galor and Weil 1996; Dreze and Sen 2002; Caldwell 1982). Of interest, women with a higher level of education not only produce less children but also "higher quality" children (Becker et al. 1990). The effects that the education of the mothers has on children's health and education in poor countries have been well outlined in the literature (Le Vine et al. 1985; Baizan and Camps 2007).

A third exogenous factor is race and ethnicity. The disparity between the demographic patterns of different races is narrowing. This pattern is seen also by the convergence of mortality rates among blacks and whites in the United States in the second half of the twentieth century (see Table 4.3), due in part to the democratization of the supply of public goods, such as water sanitation and other health services (see Troesken 2004), as well as to a degree of convergence in income levels.

We present two models in the following section. The purpose of the first is to identify relevant variables, for explaining the global evolution of fertility. Since there is a considerable disparity in the magnitude of the numerical value of certain variables the model is presented multiplying the values for fertility and infant mortality per thousand. Our second model presents variables affecting the gender gap.

The Empirical Results on Variables Affecting Fertility

Table 4.4 contains the results of regression 1, which is based on panel data for 145 countries (Barro and Lee 2013; World Bank) for which we have continuous information corresponding to every five years period from 1965 to 2010. The total number of observations is 1012 as there is a considerable amount of missing values. We avoid country fixed effects here, since some variables, such as race and ethnic fractionalization are held constant. The variables we include in this panel regression are per capita GDP, population size, infant mortality, the interaction of infant mortality with Indian race, the interaction of infant mortality with

Table 4.4 The variables affecting fertility at the world level, 1965–2010

Panel regression analysis with year fixed effects Dependent variable: Fertility rates*1000	
Per capita GDP	−0.0000191 (0.0000141)
Population	−0.000000935 (0.000000226)**
Infant Mort*1000	0.0115972 (0.0038167)***
Infant M*Indian *1000	−0.1840857 (0.16889)
Infant M*Black *1000	−0.0664981 (0.041899)*
Female education (in years of primary school)	−614.0746 (20.93335)***
Ethnic fractionalization	781.9244 (158.8337)***
Indian	15.38975 (2.304191)***
Black	10.2047 (1.104309)***
1965	−115.0131 (198.729)
1970	−374.564 (190.5099)*
1975	−666.8173 (188.6754)**
1980	−825.4787 (187.6272)***
1985	−949.4833 (187.9235)***
1990	−771.5252 (188.9998)***
1995	−1439.589 (180.2016)***
2000	−1511.638 (180.3185)***
2005	−1392.792 (184.8643)***
2010	−1374.794 (183.4817)***
Constant	6222.175 (182.8758)***

Number of observations = 1012
F (19,992) = 185.73
R^2 = 0.7535; *p 10%, **p 5%, ***p 1%
Data source Data on female human capital are from Barro and Lee (2013). Data on per capita GDP, Fertility and Infant Mortality come from the World Bank. Data on ethnicity are from Alberto Alesina's dataset. The aggregation from ethnicity to racial groups (black, Indian...) has been done aggregating Alesina's data

black population, female education, ethnic fractionalization and the effects of ethnic composition (share of Indian and blacks in the total population).

One of the table's most significant results are the very low explanatory power of income levels (per capita GDP) and the high impact of infant mortality, race, and female education. Taking into account that the dependent variable is fertility rates * 1000 the impact of income is almost nil. Based on this finding we can infer that endogenous variables, associated with economic growth (such as those shown in the diagram presented earlier, including: living standards, urbanization, internal migrations, and services supply) are unimportant in explaining the evolution of fertility in the second half of the twentieth century. That may be because minimum necessary supplies of health services and other public goods characteristic of the modern world in the twentieth century (such as water sanitation, well established transport and communication networks, basic agrarian technologies for avoiding food output and price volatility) were already in place in most (although obviously not all) countries by the time period in question. It also may be due to the world having become increasingly globalized in terms of communications and transport, meaning that the human capital factors so important to the spread of the demographic changes in Europe were already being established across the planet in the second half of the twentieth century.

If income is not relevant, which variables are really significant? According to our model, the relevant variables are those presented previously as exogenous to family formation preferences, i.e. infant mortality, female education, and race (particularly the difference between Indian, blacks and whites). An increase of one point in infant mortality rates leads to an increase of 0.012 points in fertility rates. A one-year increase in women's primary schooling causes the number of children born to fall by 0.614 (worldwide average). Fertility levels are higher among blacks and Indians relative to whites. Nonetheless, combining the variables being black or Indian with infant mortality has a negative effect on fertility levels. That may be due to extraordinary mortality caused by pandemics and civil wars in the parts of the world inhabited by blacks and Indians. Mortality due to epidemics and wars can produce an imbalance in a country's sex ratio or make it impossible for many women to have children because of the spread of diseases such as AIDS.

Based on these results, we can conclude that the way to reduce fertility levels in sub-Saharan Africa and poor countries elsewhere is to improve infant mortality rates by means of scientific and medical innovations that pave the way for the eradication of pandemics such as AIDS, HIV, and malaria. The diseases in question kill people of all ages and are a factor in people failing to act in a manner in keeping with expectations of being better off in the future. Additionally, high levels of infant mortality mean that only a limited number of the babies born actually survive the first year, leading many women to have many children to ensure that at least some of them will reach adulthood, in the hope that they will be able to support the family when their parents grow old.

Our findings also highlight the high impact of female education on fertility levels. Indeed this is the most powerful variable to explain fertility diminution in poor countries. As we already said, one year more of female primary education in poor countries leads to a diminution of 0.614 births per couple. Therefore, gender differences in the access to education and wealth may be very important to explain fertility evolution. Table 4.5 contains results related to variables affecting the gender gap worldwide and therefore factors affecting the access to education by women. In the case of this second model, we only have results for the variables involved for the year 2003, and the regression is therefore based on cross-section data across countries. Nonetheless, the results are significant, with very important implications for those seeking to control levels of fertility, as countries such as China and India have attempted in the recent past. The tables and figures presented in section "A Simple Model of the Reasons for Declining Fertility" show that fertility levels in South and East Asia fell sharply between 1960 and 2010, mainly due to family planning policies being exogenously imposed on couples. As both societies are highly biased where gender is concerned, programs like China's one-child policy have resulted in an increase in infant mortality rates of girls relative to that of boys, in sharp contrast to what is happening in the rest of the world. That is not to suggest that infanticide is

Table 4.5 Explaining the gender gap, 2003

Dependent variable = log (ppp female earnings/ppp male earnings)				
	(1)	(2)	(3)	(4)
Log per capita GDP	0.0009	−0.0228	−0.00977	−0.1752
	(0.0209)	(0.0208)	(0.0138)	(0.0155)
Log female ec.act.	1.0534	0.9619	1.0881	0.9739
	(0.0958)***	(0.1002)***	(0.0897)***	(0.0986)***
Latin America	−0.1416	−0.1685	−0.07564	−0.1658
	(0.0520)***	(0.0579)***	*(0.0542)*	(0.0529)***
East South Asia	0.0807	0.0642	0.0917	0.1107
	(0.0377)**	(0.4545)	(0.0369)***	(0.0351)***
Log education ga	−0.02971			
(years spent school)	(0.0317)			
Market openness		0.0407		
		(0.3242)		
% Indian			−0.0463	
			(0.0023)***	
Log Wom in Govern				0.0614
				(0.03510)*
Constant	−4.5697	−4.1010	−4.5976	−4.2743
	(0.4230)***	(0.4311)***	(0.3504)***	(0.3765)***
N	122	77	118	119
R^2	0.592	0.569	0.650	0.599

Source UN Human Development Report (2005)

**p* 10%, ***p* 5%, ****p* 1%

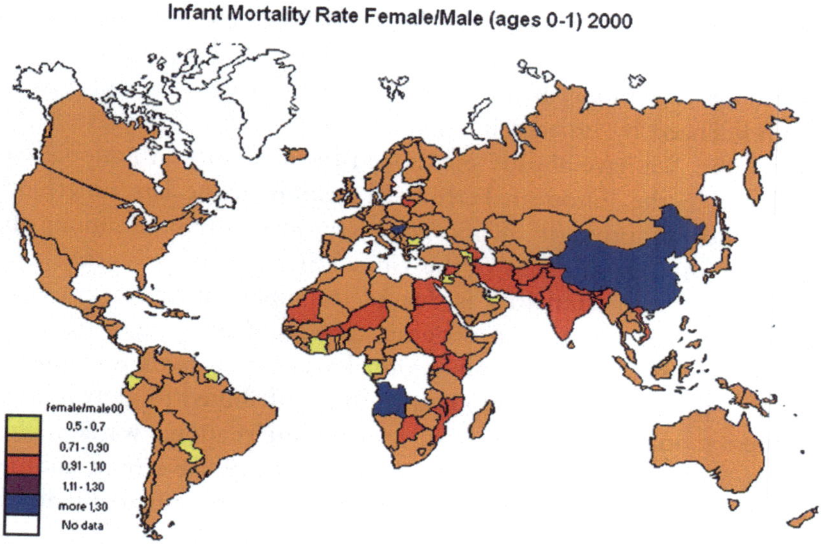

Fig. 4.4 The gender gap in infant mortality rates, 2000 (*Source* World Bank datasets)

practiced in these countries. However, if a couple wants a son but official policy restricts them to having just one child and they have a daughter the main consequence is that they seek to give her in adoption or, as in the case of Taiwan, to arrange a child marriage for her. The end result is an increase in infant mortality levels among girls relative to among boys, as several research projects demonstrate (Fig. 4.4).

Conclusion

There have been some common movements in a number of demographic variables in most parts of the world in recent years, although substantial differences in the absolute levels of those variables still remain. What is perhaps most interesting, is the similar timing of such movements in fertility and mortality rates, as well as in the various related explanatory factors such as infant mortality rates, years of schooling of women, female labor force participation, and the relevant economic factors. Such similarity in the timing of changes raises questions about the importance of country-specific factors as opposed to those influenced by broader international forces. This, of course is not a new point. We have already mentioned the similarity in national fertility levels in the European Fertility Transition in the late nineteenth century and, the similarity of movements in mortality rates among the black and white populations of the United States in the twentieth century. Whether such similarity is due to technological aspects, external effects in the communication of ideas, the spread of changes in tastes, or the direct intervention of international agencies or foreign countries, is open to debate, as is the importance to be attributed to globalization and international connections. Civil wars and international warfare, phenomena with a rather long and continuous history, have been another cause of changing fertility and mortality patterns. It is estimated that war has been responsible for over 15 million deaths in Africa in the past half century, contributing, in conjunction with diseases, a pattern of basically unchanged fertility in sub-Saharan Africa up to 1990, with only a moderate decline in the subsequent decade. The regions of sub-Saharan Africa and South Asia have the highest fertility rates, despite falls in recent years, as well as the lowest female literacy rates, and rather different female labor force participation rates. The relationship between fertility rates and the degree of inequality requires further study, but it is probable that greater inequality and higher rates of fertility are linked.

Worldwide trends in the second half of the twentieth century included an increase in the number of years of schooling received by women and in the female labor force participation rate, something that many predicted to lead to a decline in fertility because of the increased value of a woman's time and the effect this has on the cost of childbearing. That is clearly the pattern predicted for developed economies, where female labor force increases reflect an improvement in the opportunities available to women and allow for reductions in child labor to permit increased education. However, this relationship has been U-shaped (Goldin 1994), since female labor force participation is also very high when income levels are low and female and child labor is necessary to support families. In sub-Saharan Africa, where rates of female labor force activity are high and rates of female education and literacy are low, fertility rates are high, which can be interpreted as a consequence of another important variable that, according to our analysis, plays an important role in shaping fertility, namely, high rates of infant mortality. Furthermore, sub-Saharan Africa, unlike other regions, is unique in that its levels both of female labor force participation and child labor activity are high. This takes us back to the long-standing issue of policy towards developing nations. How can we determine what actions to take, who should become the major agents of change, and what is the feasible time period within which to accomplish those goals?.

Bibliography

Baizan, Pau, Camps, Enriqueta, "The Impact of Women's Educational and Economic Resources on Fertility. Spanish Birth Cohorts, 1901–1950", in *Gendering the Fertility Decline in the Western World*, edited by Angelique Janssens. New York, Peter Lang, 2007.

Barro, Robert J., Lee, John W., "International Data on Education Attainment Updates and Implications", Harvard University Working Paper Series, 2000.

Barro, Robert J., Lee, John W., "International Measures of Schooling Years and Schooling Quality", *American Economic Review. Papers and Proceedings*, 86 (2013): 218–223.

Becker, Gary S., "Quantity and Quality of Life and World Inequality", *The American Economic Review*, 95, no. 1 (2005): 277–291.

Becker, Gary S., Murphy, Kevin, Tamura, Robert F., "Human Capital, Fertility, and Economic Growth", *Journal of Public Economics*, 98, no. 5 (1990): 12–37.

Boserup, Ester, *Women's Role in Economic Development*. Hampshire, Gower, 1970.

Brown, John, Guinnane, Timothy, "Fertility Transition in a Rural Catholic Population: Bavaria 1880–1910", *Population Studies*, 56 (2002): 35–49.

Caldwell, John C., *Theory of Fertility Decline*. New York, Academic Press, 1982.

Coale, Ansley J., Watkins, Susan C. (ed.), *The Decline of Fertility in Europe*. Princeton, Princeton University Press, 1986.

De Vries, Jan, *European Urbanization*. London, Routledge, 1985.

Dreze, Jan, Sen, Amartya, *India: Development and Participation*. Cambridge, Cambridge University Press, 2002.

Fogel, Robert W., *The Escape from Hunger and Premature Death, 1700–2100: Europe, America and the Third World*. Cambridge, Cambridge University Press, 2004.

Galor, Oded, Weil, David N., "The Gender Gap, Fertility and Growth", *The American Economic Review*, 86 (1996): 374–387.

Goldin, Claudia, *Understanding the Gender Gap*. Oxford, Oxford University Press, 1990.

Goldin, Claudia, "The U Shaped Female Labor Force Function in Economic Development and Economic History", NBER Working Paper Series 4704, 1994.

Le Vine, R.A., Le Vine, S.E., et al. "Women Schooling and Child Care in the Demographic Transition: A Mexican Case Study", *Population and Development Review*, 75 (1985): 992–1015.

Sachs, Common Wealth. United Nations, Human Development Reports, various dates.

Sachs, Jeffrey D., *The End of Poverty: Economic Possibilities for Our Time*. New York, The Penguin Press, 2005.

Sachs, Jeffrey D., *Common Wealth: Economics for a Crowded Planet*. New York, Penguin Books, 2008.

Sen, Amartya, "More Than 100 Million Women Are Missing", *The New York Review*, 1990.

Sen, Amartya, "Missing Women: Social Inequality Outweighs Women's Survival Advantage in Asia and North Africa", *British Medical Journal*, 304 (1992): 587–588.

Sen, Amartya, "Missing Women Revisited: Reduction in Female Mortality Has Been Counterbalanced by Sex Selective Abortions", *British Medical Journal*, 327, no. 7427 (2003): 1297–1298.

Troesken, Werner, *Water, Race and Disease*. Cambridge, MIT Press, 2004.

Voth, Joachim, Voigtländer, Nico, "How the West 'Invented' Fertility Restriction", *American Economic Review*, 103, no. 6 (2013): 2227–2264.

Williamson, Jeffrey G., "Demographic Change, Economic Growth and Inequality", in *Population Matters*, edited by Nancy Birsdall, Allen C. Kelley, Steven W. Sinding. Oxford, Oxford University Press, 2001, pp. 106–135.

Wrigley, Edward A., *Poverty, Progress and Population*. Cambridge, Cambridge University Press, 2004.

World Bank, *World Bank Annual Reports*. Washington, DC, Various dates.

5

The Economic Geography of Human Capital in Twentieth-Century Latin America in an International Comparative Perspective

Abstract In this chapter, we present results for educational achievement in the different economic regions of Latin America (Big countries: Mexico and Brazil; Southern Cone; Andean countries; Central America; and others) during the twentieth century. The variables we use to measure education are average years of education, literacy, average years in primary school, average years in secondary school, and average years in university. To attain a broader perspective on the relationship of education with human capital and with welfare and wellbeing we relate the educational measures to life expectancy and other human capital variables and GDP per capita. We then use regressions to examine the impact of race and ethnicity on education, and of education on economic growth and levels of GDP per capita. The most significant results we wish to emphasize are related to the importance of race and racial fractionalization in explaining regional differences in educational achievement. Southern Cone countries, with a higher density of white population, present the highest levels of education in average terms, while countries from Central America and Brazil, with a higher

E. Camps-Cura, *Changes in Population, Inequality and Human Capital Formation in the Americas in the Nineteenth and Twentieth Centuries*, Palgrave Studies in Economic History, https://doi.org/10.1007/978-3-030-21351-0_5

proportion of Indigenous Americans and/or blacks, have the lowest levels. In most countries, the major improvements in educational achievement are the expansion of primary education during the first half of the twentieth century, and the expansion of secondary education after 1950. In all cases, average years in university are low, despite improvements in university quality during the last decades of the century when professors exiled during dictatorships returned to their countries of origin. International comparisons (continental averages for years of education weighted by country population size) place twentieth-century Latin America in an intermediate position between the United States and Europe at the top, and countries from Asia and Africa at the bottom.

Keywords Natural experiment · Education · Health · Endogenous · Comparative

Introduction

Historically, research into human capital shows a general consensus that its formation has been unequal among individuals and groups, within and across countries. This fact has had further consequences for patterns of economic performance. Education and human capital formation have had a large impact on economic growth through their impact on skills and the ability to innovate and diffuse innovation. The leading scholars on human capital formation (Becker 1964; Lucas 2002; Barro 2012) have considered this variable as an endogenous variable. Only when a certain level of GDP per capita was achieved could education develop further. Growth and higher incomes led to better education. But in developing countries the opposite causal relation may also be true, in which educational improvement is an exogenous variable that leads to further economic growth. A historical example of this second causal relation in Latin American countries was the spread of mass education during the "Estado Docente" years that fostered economic growth in the "Desarrollismo" period (Frankema 2009a; Arroyo-Abad 2016).

In any case, the appropriateness of education systems depends on the structure of industries and on the economic structure in general. In agrarian societies and in societies where industries only developed the technologies of the first industrial revolution, education has played just a minor part in economic growth, having a lesser role than that of health, physical strength and height, as has been recently empirically shown for Spain (Camps 2016).

On the other hand, the spread of education also depends on educational and income inequality (Batten and Mumme 2010; Alvaredo and Gasparini 2015). Recent results for developing countries show that in the late twentieth century, from 1970 to 2010, within-country income inequality showed a slight increase while levels of poverty decreased sharply (Sala-i-Martin 2006; Alvaredo and Gasparini 2015). According to Sala-i-Martin (2006), the period 1970–2000 was also one of economic convergence in world equality. Inequality sharply diminished across countries thanks to economic growth of developing countries, mainly the world's most highly populated countries of South and East Asia.

Income inequality has additional effects on educational performance. People belonging to the highest income percentiles of the population can afford to pay more for education and do not depend on labor by their children, so they can further develop their skills while people from the lowest percentiles cannot. Nonetheless, there is an intergenerational effect in this relation. Parents' incomes influence education and, in turn, their children's incomes (Balcazar et al. 2015, see also Baizan and Camps 2007 for the influence of father's income and mother's education levels on their children's education in twentieth-century Spain). On the other hand, the educational supply and amount of education an individual can afford will depend on the social and ethnic group they belong to. With regard to the effect of race and ethnicity, recent studies demonstrate the importance of segmentation of the educational supply according to race. While in some cases this kind of inequality has tended to diminish in the last decades of the twentieth century (Engerman and Sokoloff 2012; Camps and Engerman 2016; Bucciferro 2014). racial and ethnic discrimination in access to education has major repercussions on the incomes, wages, and occupations of ethnic group members.

In this paper, we analyze the economic geography of human capital (education and health) in twentieth-century Latin America with special reference to education. In order to make feasible comparisons we group Latin American countries into economic regions: Big countries—Mexico and Brazil; the Southern Cone; Andean countries; Central America, and others (see the Appendix for the details of the countries in each group). In terms of economic geography, only Southern Cone countries belong to the temperate climate area, while most of the other countries belong to the tropical area with the corresponding economic growth outcomes (tropical epidemics, high temperatures that yield good returns in production, and negative environmental effects). We think that while these economic regions share a lot of common characteristics in terms of social organization, ethnic identity and culture are important when explaining human capital evolution.

In order to present the first results, based on the educational structure, we need to consider the quantity of education (average years of schooling) versus the quality of schooling (e.g. expenditure on schooling). While we were able to collect most of these variables in quantitative terms we have had to rely on the available literature regarding its quality (Reimers 2006; Frankema 2009b; Bertola O'Campo 2013; Valente and Berry 2015). In the figures and tables in the Appendix, we also present performance according to education levels: primary (elementary, grades 1–8) leading to the improvement of literacy levels and basic knowledge; secondary (high school, grades 9–12); and tertiary (university levels). These education stages are sequential and, therefore, more years of schooling means higher levels of education.

We must also consider that how much education individuals receive does not strictly depend only on personal choice, at least in developing countries. They are subject to constraints such as income level, parental income, urban or rural residence, and gender (Balcazar et al. 2015). They also depend on legislative and judicial influences that may or may not foster the enforcement of education, such as government spending at different levels (state, local, federal), what amount is compulsory and for how many years, and subsidies for potential students (Engerman and Sokoloff 2012; Engerman and Camps 2016; Balcazar et al. 2015). Last but not least, education is also influenced by suffrage, and the number of overseas migrants (Alvaredo and Gasparini 2015).

Data Sources and Methodology

In this paper, we use the main variables to measure human capital, levels of education and information on GDP per capita. Data on human capital are from the dataset led by Jan Luiten Van Zanden, Clio Infra. Data on levels of education are from Barro and Lee (2013) and data on GDP per capita are from the last results presented by the Maddison group.

Measuring the impact of human capital on economic growth is a complex task since this variable is endogenous. This is why in the last part of the paper we present a natural experiment based on a reduced sample of Latin American countries. But quantitative results for all countries are presented in Sect. 2 of the paper.

The Evolution of Human Capital During the Twentieth Century in Quantitative Terms

In the figures and tables in the Appendix, we present the data on the evolution of human capital variables, in terms of both education and health, in Latin American countries. Tables in the Appendix also present results based on the international comparison, at the continental level, of educational achievement weighted by country population size. An initial result that should be stressed is that during the twentieth century all human capital variables improved throughout Latin America. All variables related to schooling (years of education, educational Ginis, illiteracy, years in primary school, years in secondary school, years in university) and health (height, life expectancy) improved in all Latin American countries. The levels in 1900 were low, so there was much room for improvement, but the importance of this result is nevertheless worth highlighting. In spite of periods of bad economic conditions, economic indebtedness and other factors leading to economic turmoil (dictatorships, foreign emigration, etc.) the expansion of human capital was dramatic between 1900 and 2000. We will first examine the basic data on schooling, literacy, and educational Ginis; then proceed to the analysis of education levels, and also discuss changes in health.

In Figs. 5.1, 5.2, and 5.3, we present the results for the main variables representing the development of education.

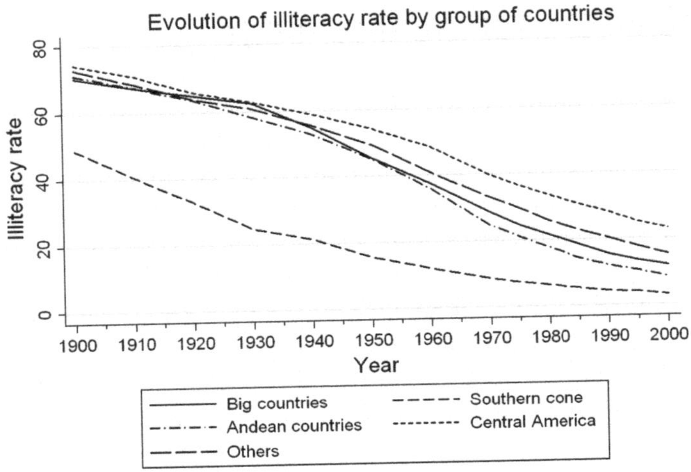

Fig. 5.1 Illiteracy rates in the regions of Latin America, 1900–2000

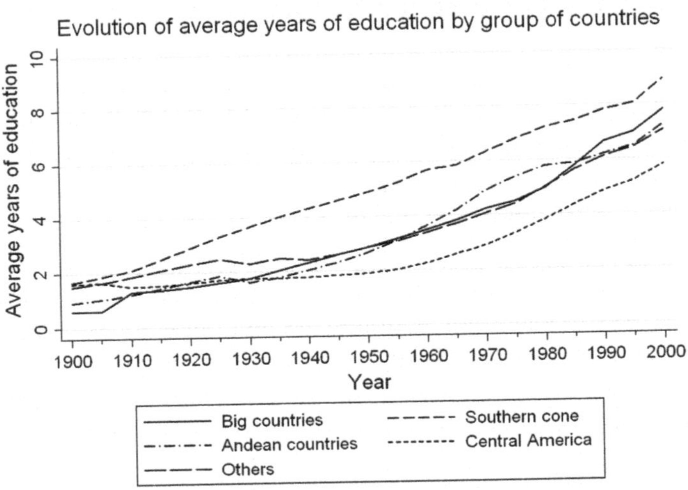

Fig. 5.2 Years of schooling in the regions of Latin America, 1900–2000

In these figures, we see a common trend, independent of income levels and in all economic regions, of a diminution in illiteracy levels, an increase in average years of education, and a decrease in the educational Gini. With the exception of Southern Cone countries, which

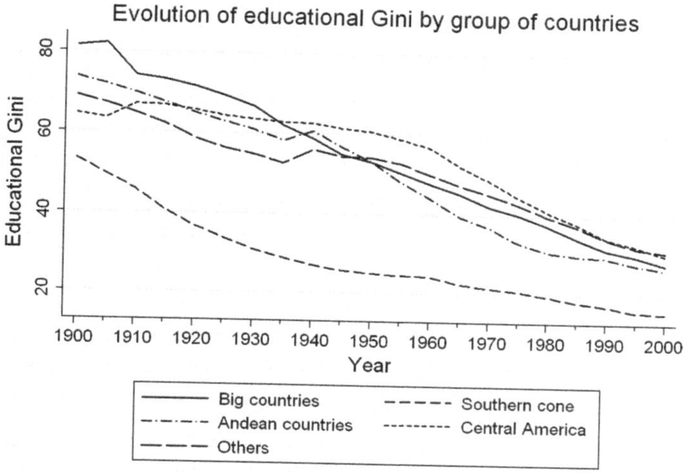

Fig. 5.3 Educational Inequality in the regions of Latin America, 1900–2000

have been the most successful, in all other economic regions illiteracy levels diminish from around 70% in 1900 to levels around 20–40% in 2000; average years of education increase from 1 or 2 in 1900 to 5–7 in 2000. As illiteracy decreased and education expanded, the educational Gini diminished from 60–80% in 1900 to 30–40% in 2000 (5% in the Southern Cone). Southern Cone countries had been in a better situation during the nineteenth century. Since these countries received most of the European migration to Latin America already during the last third of the nineteenth century, they had the highest density of urban white population and maintained their position in relation to other Latin American regions in the twentieth century.

We present the results for each education level from 1950 to 2000. The years of education in primary schools have the greatest impact on illiteracy rates. Figure 5.1 indicates that, with the exception of Southern Cone countries, illiteracy rates were higher than the other countries in Latin America during most of the twentieth century. In spite of the fact that years in primary school show an upward trend, by the year 2000 they were less than four years in most countries, but five years in the Southern Cone. This means that throughout the twentieth century a large percentage of children did not complete primary education. Course repetitions and dropouts were frequent experiences that can explain the low number of years spent in primary school in most countries.

Years in secondary school and university show similar outcomes. Southern Cone and Andean countries have the best performance, while Central America and the Big countries do the worst. Notice, in particular, that the average years of education in universities is less than one in all country groups, meaning that university attendance was poorly achieved, at least till the end of the twentieth century.

When we consider the evolution of other variables regarding human capital, including health variables, we again observe the superiority of Southern Cone countries. This group of countries consistently has not only the lowest illiteracy rates and lowest educational Gini, but also the highest life expectancy, tallest average height, and highest average years of education at primary, secondary and university levels. At the opposite end of the spectrum, Central America, with the highest proportion of blacks and/or indigenous Americans, has the highest illiteracy rate, lowest life expectancy, smallest heights, and, until the 1990s, the lowest enrollment rates in all three educational levels and the smallest decline in the educational Gini.

Thus the most striking differences are between the Southern Cone and Central America. Big countries (Mexico and Brazil) have a large growth in height and GDP per capita (see Table 5.1), average years of education, and a relatively large decline in the educational Gini. Andean and other countries range somewhere around the middle.

We obtained similar results regarding the timing of the improvements observed in the figures and tables in the Appendix. The earliest improvements began in Southern Cone countries, who lead in average years of education by 50 years, in primary education by 20 years, in the upswing in GDP per capita by 20–50 years; and in the increase in life expectancy by 10 years.

These figures show that there are many issues that come into play regarding the nature of human capital in Latin American countries. Nonetheless, we can draw the conclusion that during the twentieth century there was a general trend of human capital improvement across all countries, although racial segmentation still exists. The standard of the education supplied to non-white populations from rural areas clearly needs further improvement.

The Role of Race and Ethnicity in Educational Attainment

There is a long history of ethnic and racial segregation in Latin America, which basically starts with the settlement by white Europeans mostly from Spain and Portugal but also from the Netherlands, Britain, and France. The initial settlement in lands in which Native-American Indians were resident, often led to assaults by Europeans to take land and to relocate the indigenous peoples. The arrival of Europeans diseases previously not known to the indigenous peoples of Latin America, led to a series of severe epidemics that resulted in a significant population decrease estimated by some to be about 80% within two centuries. The major outcome was that their social and political power was limited, and the lack of suffrage was reflected in lowered political influence, leading to fewer social services, including education. In several Latin American countries, a limited labor supply to produce export commodities led to the importation of black slaves from Africa. Over time this led to a large number of African-American slaves in Brazil, Venezuela, Cuba, and Colombia. After the nineteenth century abolitions of slavery, the ex-slave and the free new black population were not granted rights to benefit from education, and were restricted economically and politically by various legal and non-legal policies. These restrictions led to a much lower amount of schooling than for whites, as well as lower expenditures for schools and schooling than for whites in both rural and urban areas. Even after legislation to end this pattern in the second part of the twentieth century, differentials in the quantity and quality of education remained. Attempts in some nations to improve the situation of the indigenous populations led to some, but still limited, improvements.

Racial groups can be basically divided into two groups: whites (of different nationalities, native-born and migrants) and nonwhites (Native Americans—indigenous peoples—and African-Americans who came to the Americas as slaves). In terms of racial composition, we can group Latin American countries as follows:

a. Majority white (50% or more): Costa Rica, Brazil, Uruguay, Argentina, and Chile (the latter being 47.4% whites while Indigenous Americans plus Mestizos equalled 52.6%, so that whites have not a clear majority).
b. Majority Indigenous American and Mestizos: Mexico, Guatemala, Honduras, Nicaragua, Panama, Colombia, Ecuador, Peru, Bolivia, and Paraguay.
c. Over 20% black: Colombia, Venezuela, and Brazil.

In order to estimate the impact of race on education and per capita GDP we present the following regressions.

In Table 5.1, we only obtain statistically significant results for the year 2000, but the value and sign of the coefficient leave little doubt as to the positive causal relation between percent white, education levels, and per capita GDP. Signs for Indigenous peoples are negative in 1950 and positive in 2000 but are not statistically significant. The coefficient for blacks is negative in both 1950 and 2000. These results demonstrate the inequality with regard to racial composition for both education and GDP per capita.

To further examine the results in Table 5.1, we have recalculated the regression in Table 5.2 where the values of years of schooling and per capita GDP are the average values of each country in the first and then the second halves of the century. Again the values and signs of the coefficients provide the same information as in Table 5.1, although in this case we only obtain statistically significant results in the relationship between percentage white and per capita GDP.

To further explore the relationship between race, school attainment and per capita GDP growth we conducted a natural experiment with a sample of countries that had a similar evolution before the cutoff line of 1890. The treatment countries are the Southern Cone countries, Argentina and Chile, with a majority white population, and the control

Table 5.1 Race, education and GDP per capita

	1950		2000	
	Average years of education	ln GDP	Average years of education	ln GDP
Indian	−0.002	−0.004	0.021	0.001
	(0.017)	(0.007)	(0.017)	(0.006)
White	0.018	0.007	0.027**	0.010**
	(0.011)	(0.004)	(0.010)	(0.004)
Black	−0.026	−0.029	−0.023	−0.014**
	(0.071)	(0.028)	(0.015)	(0.006)
Constant	2.575***	7.652***	6.269***	8.128***
	(0.702)	(0.274)	(0.575)	(0.225)
Observations	17	17	20	20
R^2	0.240	0.333	0.494	0.556

Standard errors in parentheses. Omitted category is race mixed
*$p < 0.1$, **$p<0.05$, ***$p<0.01$

Table 5.2 Race, education and GDP per capita

	(1)	(2)	(3)	(4)
	Mean education	Mean edu	Mean lgdp	Mean lgdp
Indian	−0.126	−0.010	−0.044	−0.005
	(0.189)	(0.020)	(0.051)	(0.006)
White	0.156	0.010	0.047*	0.006*
	(0.099)	(0.013)	(0.027)	(0.004)
Black	−0.363	−0.042	0.038	−0.022
	(1.226)	(0.081)	(0.330)	(0.023)
Constant	1.943	3.709***	6.934***	7.783***
	(4.251)	(0.845)	(1.146)	(0.243)
Observations	33	33	33	33
R^2	0.214		0.237	
Fixed effects	Yes	No	Yes	No

Standard errors in parentheses. Omitted category is race mixed
There are two observations for each country: the average values in the first and second half of the twentieth century, respectively
*$p < 0.1$, **$p < 0.05$, ***$p < 0.01$

countries are Brazil (more than 20% black), and Colombia and Peru, with a majority of indigenous peoples and mestizos. As a result, we want to stress the differences between whites and nonwhites with regard to the impact of racial composition on education and per capita GDP growth.

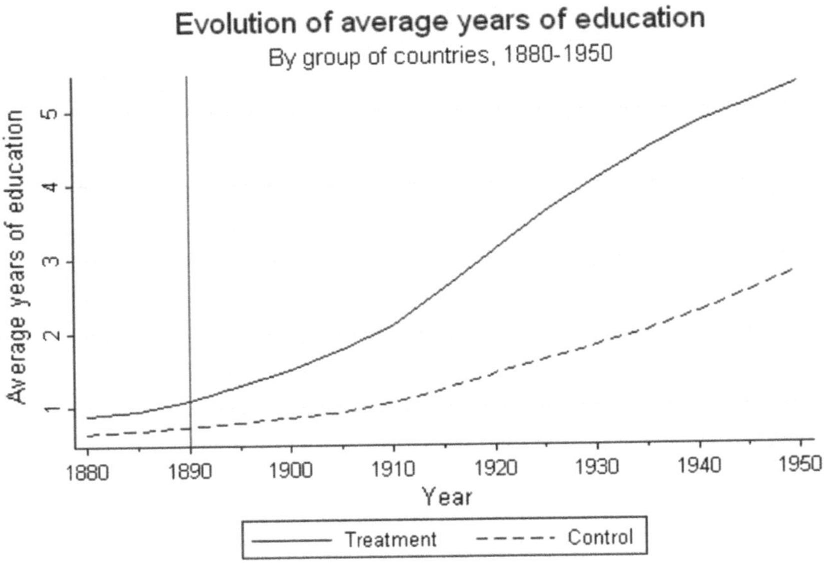

Fig. 5.4 Evolution of average years of education applying Diff-in-Diff model

Treatment countries are Argentina and Chile and control countries Brazil, Colombia, and Peru. As Fig. 5.4 illustrates, there are noteworthy educational differences between the treatment countries (Argentina and Chile) and the control countries (Brazil, Colombia, and Peru), the increase in education being far greater in treatment countries, as was previously demonstrated in part 3 of this paper.

Table 5.3 presents the results of our Diff-in-Diff analysis, in which we regress the average years of education on a dummy in the treatment group (i.e. group 1 countries), a dummy post (equal to 1 after 1890, 0 otherwise) and the interaction between the two. The last column includes the whole sample while the other columns are for different subperiods. We can see that the implementation of primary schooling up to 1890 had a positive effect on average years of schooling where it was applied, as the Treat × Post coefficient is positive and significant.

Table 5.4 shows the results for the estimation of the relationship between education and per capita GDP, and also the regression of GDP per capita in our previous Diff-in-Diff model as an instrumental variable

Table 5.3 Primary schooling laws and education—Diff-in-Diff

Average years of education					
	(1)	(2)	(3)	(4)	(5)
Treat	0.297	0.297	0.297	0.297	0.297
	(0.201)	(0.257)	(0.415)	(0.537)	(1.121)
Post	0.291*	0.370*	0.629**	0.939**	2.564***
	(0.161)	(0.199)	(0.303)	(0.380)	(0.756)
Treat × Post	0.592**	0.723**	1.123**	1.402**	1.556
	(0.254)	(0.315)	(0.480)	(0.601)	(1.195)
Constant	0.661***	0.661***	0.661**	0.661*	0.661
	(0.127)	(0.162)	(0.263)	(0.340)	(0.709)
Observations	40	45	60	75	125
R^2	0.594	0.555	0.503	0.483	0.291
Sample	1880–1915	1880–1920	1880–1935	1880–1950	1880–2000

Standard errors in parentheses
Treatment group countries are Argentina and Chile, while control group countries are Brazil, Colombia and Peru
$^*p < 0.1$, $^{**}p < 0.05$, $^{***}p < 0.01$

Table 5.4 Education and GDP per capita—IV results

	Ln of GDP per capita				
	(1)	(2)	(3)	(4)	(5)
Average years of education	0.409*	0.276	0.070	−0.009	−0.160
	(0.226)	(0.173)	(0.130)	(0.133)	(0.309)
Post	−0.000	0.075	0.312**	0.519**	1.455
	(0.136)	(0.130)	(0.157)	(0.220)	(1.013)
Treat	0.947***	0.987***	1.048***	1.071***	1.116**
	(0.164)	(0.147)	(0.161)	(0.204)	(0.539)
Constant	6.246***	6.334***	6.470***	6.522***	6.622***
	(0.130)	(0.098)	(0.079)	(0.092)	(0.233)
Observations	40	45	60	75	125
R^2	0.899	0.905	0.857	0.753	
Sample	1880–1915	1880–1920	1880–1935	1880–1950	1880–2000

Standard errors in parentheses
Treatment group countries are Argentina and Chile, while control group countries are Brazil, Colombia and Peru
$*p < 0.1$, $**p < 0.05$, $***p < 0.01$

of years of education. The last column includes the entire sample while the rest include different subperiods. We can see that the impact of education on the growth in per capita GDP is positive and significant in most cases, although the results are not as robust as for education. As a general conclusion, however, we can see that in Latin American countries the gains observed in education, which are more pronounced in the treatment group, had a positive effect on per capita GDP growth.

We conclude from our natural experiment that the implementation of measures to foster education up to 1890 had a positive effect on the evolution of education during the twentieth century being Southern Cone countries the leaders of this process. The growth in educational attainment had further consequences for economic growth. We were able to avoid the effect of the endogeneity of education by means of a Diff-in-Diff model that provided us with the instrument for the regression in Table 5.4. Increased education, especially in the treatment group, leads to growth in per capita GDP.

Latin America's Education Attainment in an International Comparative Perspective

In Tables 5.12 and 5.13 of the Appendix, we present the results of educational variables at the continental level for years 1950–2000. The results are weighted by country population size. As we can see in these tables, all educational variables improved for all continents from 1950 to 2000, independently of their income levels. The growth path in Latin America shows a period of convergence in educational variables, which is consistent with the global convergence across the world (Sala-i-Martin). It is also consistent with the trend outlined in the introduction of a decrease in the percentage of the population living in poverty. This worldwide movement after the ending of World War II came at a time of decolonization and extended international cooperation in most parts of the world.

In this context of the convergence and global increase in educational levels, Latin America holds an intermediate position between countries of Europe and North America, at the top, and countries of Asia and Africa, at the bottom (Figs. 5.5, 5.6, 5.7, 5.8, 5.9, and 5.10).

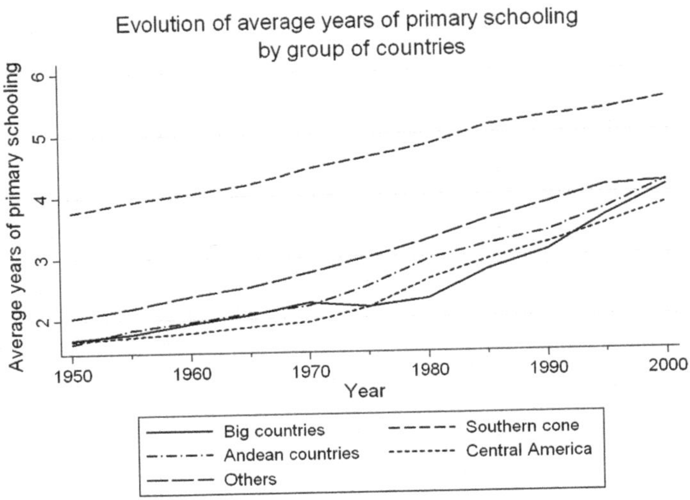

Fig. 5.5 Primary schooling in the regions of Latin America, 1950–2000

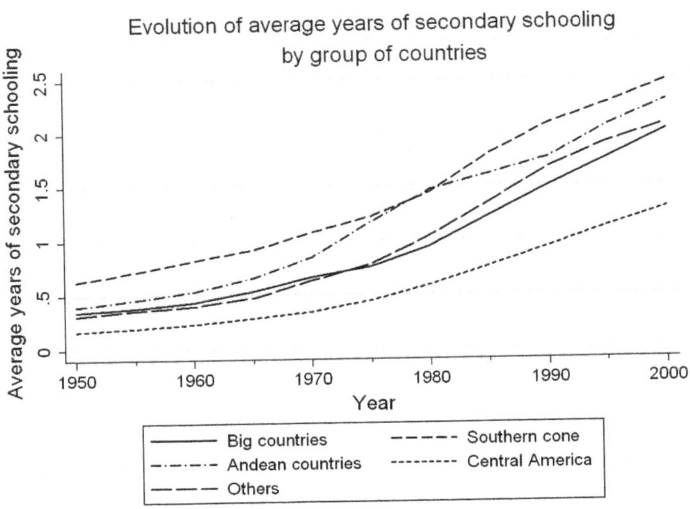

Fig. 5.6 Secondary schooling in the regions of Latin America, 1950–2000

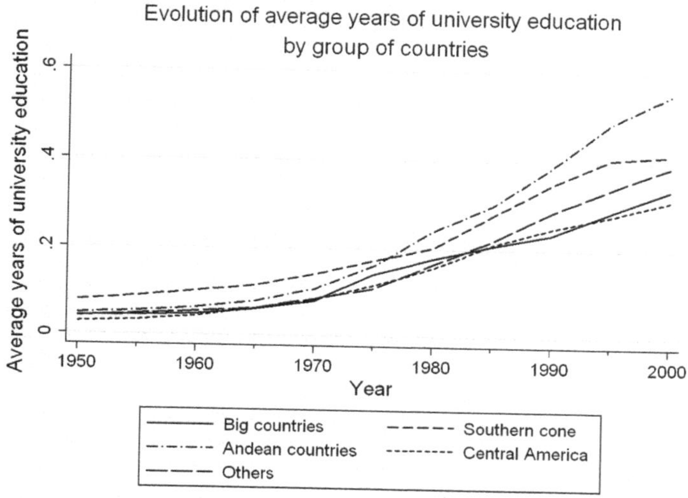

Fig. 5.7 Average years in university in the regions of Latin America, 1950–2000

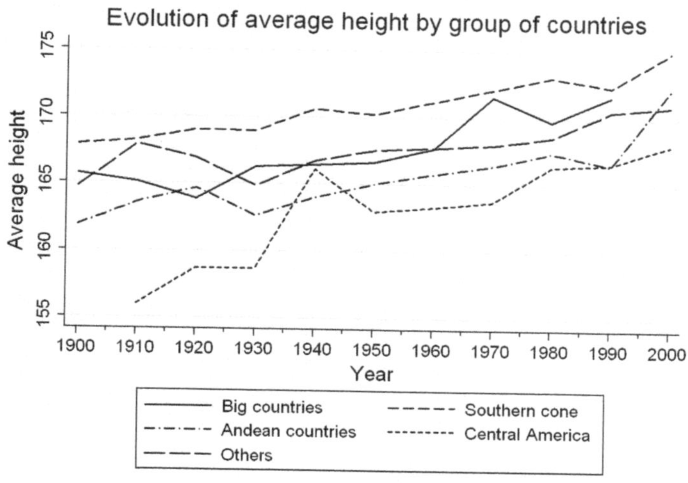

Fig. 5.8 Height in the regions of Latin America, 1900–2000

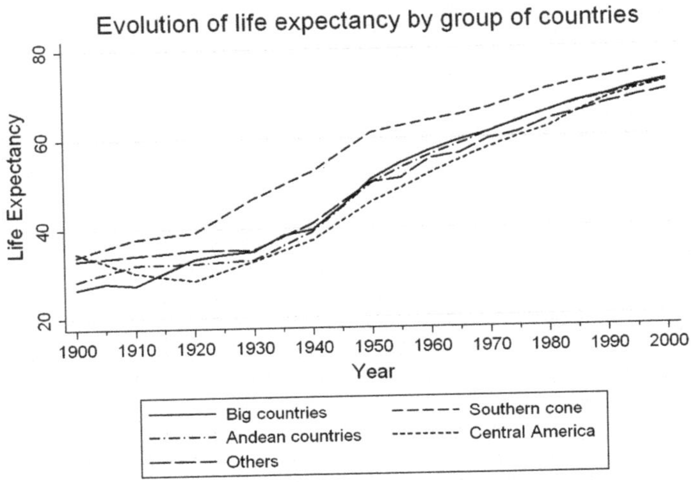

Fig. 5.9 Life expectancies in the regions of Latin America, 1900–2000

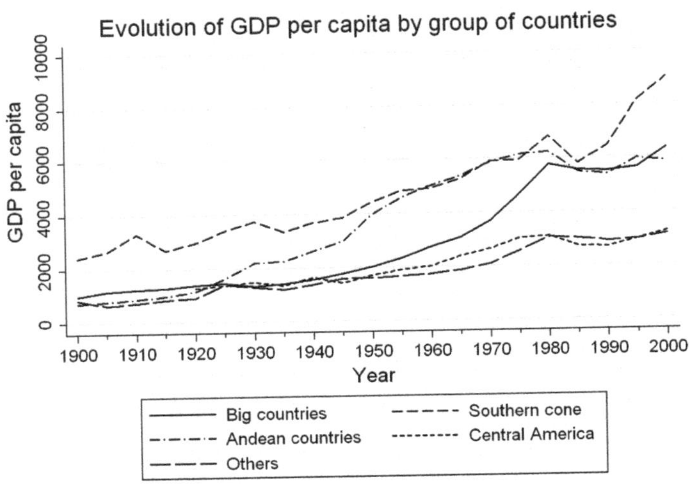

Fig. 5.10 GDP per capita in the regions of Latin America, 1900–2000

Conclusions

The twentieth century saw major improvements throughout Latin America in educational attainment, as well as in several measures of health and GDP per capita. These positive developments were also found in most parts of the world, although with some differences in timing, rates of change, and levels at the end of the twentieth century. Thus, despite variations in political, economic, and social occurrences, certain basic changes in society were not unique to Latin America, but rather were responses to certain worldwide changes in ideology and belief. Why these occurred throughout the world at this time still remains something of a mystery.

Latin American changes were not uniform although all nations experienced improvements in educational attainment, per capita GDP, life expectancies, and health. The nations of the Sothern Cone—Argentina, Uruguay, and Chile, with their majority white populations ranked the highest in all measures at the start and at the end of the period, while those in Central America, with a generally large share of its population composed of indigenous peoples did worse. In terms of educational attainment, as measured by average years of education, Central America, and, frequently Brazil and Mexico, with large populations of black and indigenous peoples were generally below the levels of other Latin American nations. While the educational performance of these non-white populations increased over time they remained relatively low. Thus the direct and indirect impact of having a large non-white population has had, and still does have, a negative impact upon the quantity, quality, and equitable distribution of education. While much attention has long been given to racial inequalities in the United States, this remains a problem to be confronted throughout Latin America, which still suffers as does the United States, from problems of racial discrimination and segregation despite a recent series of legislative, executive, and judicial attempts to end them.

Appendix

See Appendix Tables 5.5, 5.6, 5.7, 5.8, 5.9, 5.10, 5.11, 5.12, and 5.13.

Table 5.5 Year 2000

	(1)	(2)	(3)	(4)	(5)
GDP per capita	6346.465	8983.243	5840.357	3240.83	4518.676
Life expectancy	72.225	75.146	71.312	70.989	69.625
Educational Gini	28.089	15.518	26.807	30.546	30.811
Average years of education	7.785	8.896	7.242	5.786	7.596
Illiteracy	12	3.06	8.333	23	15.28
Average years in primary school	4.09	5.529	4.181	3.817	4.162
Average years in secondary school	2.009	2.468	2.285	1.287	2.065
Average years in university	0.33	0.415	0.551	0.312	0.389

Table 5.6 Year 1950

	(1)	(2)	(3)	(4)	(5)
GDP per capita	2018.371	4438.621	3947.144	1693.2	1592.999
Life expectancy	49.266	60.64	48.51	44.541	48.836
Educational Gini	53.122	25.175	53.166	60.614	54.260
Average years of education	2.857	4.884	2.662	1.898	2.863
Illiteracy	45.5	15.8	45.333	54.4	49.571
Average years in primary school	1.676	3.748	1.617	1.657	2.029
Average years in secondary school	0.350	0.630	0.400	0.171	0.315
Average years in university	0.040	0.076	0.046	0.027	0.039

Table 5.7 Year 1900

	(1)	(2)	(3)	(4)	(5)
GDP per capita	998.543	2429.321	728.0142		867.1942
Life expectancy	26.65	34.025		34.7	33.112
Educational Gini	81.390	53.313	73.62	64.575	68.958
Average years of education	0.624	1.668	0.933	1.618	1.504
Illiteracy	70.50	49.00	71.33	74.5	73.0

Values = average values for each country group
GDP per capita = in 1990 $
We have many other variables

Table 5.8 Elasticities of GDP per capita with respect to the average years of schooling

(Log GDP per capita/Log Average years of schooling)					
Year 1900	−13.83	16.569	6.5368		11.915
Year 1950	7.594	5.362	9.463	12.614	−44.7737
Year 2000	4.262	4.173	4.387	4.576	4.2224

Table 5.9 Year 2000

	Asia	Latin America	Africa	North America	Europe	Australia, Malaysia, Indonesia
Average years of education	6.58	7.11	4.08	11.95	10.06	8.17
Average years in primary school	3.61	4.66	2.85	5.83	5.76	5.07
Average years in secondary school	2.57	2.11	1.13	4090	3.69	2.66
Average years in university	0.38	0.34	0.09	1.21	0.69	0.43

Table 5.10 Year 1950*

	Asia	Latin America	Africa	North America	Europe	Australia, Malaysia, Indonesia
Average years of education	1.9	2.92	0.88	7.76	4.88	3.59
Average years in primary school	1.32	2.52	0.74	5.06	4.10	2.63
Average years in secondary school	0.53	0.34	0.12	2.34	0.69	0.87
Average years in university	0.06	0.04	0.01	0.34	0.08	0.08

*1950 may be a bad year due to WWII

Table 5.11 Year 1960

	Asia	Latin America	Africa	North America	Europe	Australia, Malaysia, Indonesia
Average years of education	2.33	3.31	1.07	8.48	5.42	4.12
Average years in primary school	1.56	2.79	0.90	5.23	4.40	2.96
Average years in secondary school	0.68	0.45	0.14	2.78	0.92	1.05
Average years in university	0.07	0.061	0.01	0.46	0.10	0.10

Table 5.12 Results weighted by population size

Year 2000	Asia	Latin America	Africa	North America	Europe	Australia, Malaysia, Indonesia
Average years of education	5.89	6.69	4.25	12.72	10.14	6.11
Average years in primary school	3.81	4.30	2.94	5.91	5.4	4.12
Average years in secondary school	1.83	2.03	1.2	5.30	3.9	1.69
Average years in university	0.25	0.35	0.11	1.50	0.72	0.28

Table 5.13 Year 1950

	Asia	Latin America	Africa	North America	Europe	Australia, Malaysia, Indonesia
Average years of education	1.2	2.5	0.90	8.07	4.83	1.84
Average years in primary school	0.97	2.1	0.74	5.09	4.30	1.40
Average years in secondary school	0.20	0.36	0.14	2.65	0.68	0.39
Average years in university	0.02	0.04	0.016	0.41	0.07	0.05

Country groups:

1. *Big countries*: Mexico, Brazil.
2. *Southern Cone*: Argentina, Chile, Uruguay.
3. *Andean countries*: Colombia, Peru, Venezuela.
4. *Central America*: Costa Rica, El Salvador, Guatemala, Honduras, Nicaragua.
5. *Others*: Bolivia, Ecuador, Panama, Republica Dominicana and others.

Average Years of schooling: population aged 15 and more.

Bibliography

Alvaredo, Facundo, Gasparini, Leonardo, "Recent Trends in Inequality and Poverty in Developing Countries", in *Handbook of Income Distribution* [ebook], edited by Anthony B. Atkinson, Francois Bourguignon, vol. II. Amsterdam, Elsevier, 2015.

Arroyo-Abad, L., "Limits to Estado Docente", *Revista de Historia Económica. Journal of Iberian and Latin American Economic History*, 34, no. 1 (2016): 81–109.

Baizan, P., Camps, E., "The Impact of Women's Educational and Economic Resources on Fertility. Spanish Birth Cohorts, 1901–1950", in *Gendering the Fertility Decline in the Western World*, edited by A. Janssens. Bern, Peter Lang, 2007.

Balcazar, C.F., Narayan, A., Tiwari, S., "Born with a Silver Spoon: Inequality in Educational Achievement Across the World", Policy Research Working Paper, 7152, World Bank Group, January 2015.

Barro, R.J., "Human Capital and Growth", *American Review Papers and Proceedings*, 113, no. 2 (May 2012).

Barro, R.J., Lee, J.W., "A New Data Set of Educational Attainment in the World, 1950–2010", *Journal of Development Economics*, 104C (2013): 184–198.

Batten, J., Mumme, Christina, "Educational Inequality from 15th to 20th Centuries", *Revistade Historia Económica. Journal of Iberian and Latin American Economic History*, no. 2 (2010).

Becker, G.S., *Human Capital: A Theoretical and Empirical Analysis with Special Reference to Education*. New York, Columbia University Press, 1964.

Bertola, L., O'Campo, J.A., *El desarrollo económica de América Latina desde la Independencia*. México, Fondo de Cultura Económica, 2013.

Bucciferro, J., "Race and Brazilian Inequality in the Lon Run", Paper presented at the Conference Latin American Inequality in the Lon Run, Buenos Aires, December 2014.

Camps, E., "The Impact of Investment in Human Capital on Economic Development. An Empirical Exercise Based on Height and Years of Schooling in Spain (1881–1998)," Economic UPF Working Papers, 2016.

Camps, E., Engerman, S., "The Impact of Race and Inequality on Human Capital Formation in Latin America During 19th and 20th Centuries", Barcelona Graduate School of Economics Working Papers Series, 2016.

Engerman, S., Sokoloff, K., *Economic Development in the Americas Since 1500: Endowments and Institutions*. New York and Cambridge, University Press-NBER, 2012.

Frankema, E., "Expansion of Mass Education", *Revista de Historia Económica. Journal of Iberian and Latin American Economic History*, 27, no. 3 (2009a): 359–396.

Frankema, E., *Has Latin America Always Been Unequal? A Comparative Study of Asset and Income Inequality in the Long 20th Century*. Leiden, Koninklijke, 2009b.

Lucas, R.E., *Lectures of Economic Growth*. Cambridge, MA, Harvard University Press, 2002.

Reimers, F., "Education for Social Progress", in *The Cambridge Economic History of Latin America*, edited by V. Blumer-Thomas, J. Coatsworth, J. Cortés Conde, vol. 2. New York, Cambridge University Press, 2006, pp. 427–480.

Sala-i-Martin, X., "The World Distribution of Income: Falling Poverty and Convergence Period", *Quarterly Journal of Economics*, 121, no. 2 (May 2006).

Valente, R.R., Berry, B.J.L., "Countering Inequality: Brazil Movimento Sem-Terra", *Geogaphical Review*, 105, no. 3 (July 2015): 1–20.

6

Education and Children's Work: Spain, Latin America, and Developing Countries

Abstract We already stressed that the twentieth century has significantly been labeled as the human capital century, specially in North America. In this chapter we focus on Latin America in a more widely comparative perspective with other developing countries and the previous metropolis, Spain. We focus on key aspects of women and child labor market participation levels and education. While in developed regions of Spain the increase of levels of education of women and children was a process that modestly began during the nineteenth century and took place during all the twentieth century, in developing countries and more precisely in Latin America the process of educational reform was slow and began in the twentieth century. Uneducated mothers with low levels of income conceived uneducated children that were soon part of the labor force, particularly in unskilled occupations of the informal sector of the economy. But in the Latin American case there is a trend towards the improvement of women's and children's condition during the last third of the twentieth century. The increase of levels of education of women brought with it the decline of levels of participation of

E. Camps-Cura, *Changes in Population, Inequality and Human Capital Formation in the Americas in the Nineteenth and Twentieth Centuries*, Palgrave Studies in Economic History, https://doi.org/10.1007/978-3-030-21351-0_6

children and the improvement of demographic conditions (infant mortality and fertility) as we already stressed in Chapter 4.

Keywords Children's work · Female education · Informal sector of the economy · Infant mortality · Domestic chores

Introduction: The Human Capital Transition

Laboring families, on the side of labor supply, and firm's labor preferences on the side of labor demand can explain the reasons why children work in different scenarios. On the side of the family, and during the demographic transition, children's work represented a very flexible asset providing security in unstable worlds (Basu and Hoang Van 1998). They allowed their parents to confront adverse economic situations caused by the business cycle (like the rise of unemployment in the formal economy) or the family cycle (this was the case when parents were growing old and they had to rely on their children as the main source of income of the family economy).

On the side of the demand for children's labor, in backward societies, such as nineteenth-century Spain or current developing countries, firms had a preference for cheap (in absolute terms) economic resources and production factors without making the economic calculation of their opportunity cost and productivity yields. Training children through the apprenticeship system was the alternative that the factory provided to formal education necessary to acquire the skills to deal with factory or farm work. By means of the apprenticeship system children learnt the know-how of industrious factory skills, dexterity and discipline and adaptation to the firm hierarchy. On the other hand, children, the same as women, were less conflictive than adult men. In the Catalan context, riots and strikes caused by trade unions to fight against low wages intensified the use of women and children instead of adult men. This choice came together with the change of location of the industries themselves that moved from urban ports such as Barcelona (points of arrival of the British coal) to rural settings that could make use of the free energy of water and where male trade unions were absent (Camps 2011; García-Balañà 2004; Llonch 2004).

While during the nineteenth century geography of industry has been considered very dependent on natural resources and coal, at the beginnings of twentieth century the spread of the second technological revolution brought with it increasing demands of education and human capital both on the side of employers and employees. Endogenous theories of growth began to apply in the sense that labor ceased to be a production factor per se, but also owned capital, human capital, which in turn increased a lot of levels of labor productivity.

In backward societies the beginnings of the human capital century (Goldin and Katz 2008) put into operation several shocks that affected the family size and composition and also the rationale of laboring families. More expensive education and training of children who postponed the age of entry into the labor market affected the family budget restriction and a "trade-off" between "quantity (i.e., fertility levels) and quality (i.e., levels of education)" of children was put into operation. Fertility levels diminished while children who in the Catalan scenarios of the nineteenth century began to work at the age of 7 postponed this vital event to the age of 12 at the beginnings of the twentieth century when they had completed mandatory primary school. Or to put it in other words, in the new situation there were less children that had attained higher levels of education. This may have had very clear effects on productivity levels. It was an engine stimulating growth of capita GDP as a consequence of human capital accumulation and also a result of lower demographic pressure on economic resources relative to the situation when fertility levels were very high (Camps and Engerman 2014). The question we want to answer here is how this process begins.

A Model of the Transition to the Human Capital Century in Spain

Recent research on developing countries has stressed the role of literate and skilled working mothers in this trade-off between the "quantity and quality" of children. In the Spanish case Baizan and Camps (2006) could identify, by means of a longitudinal analysis of the vital events of women from the cohorts of birth 1900–1950, that the education levels of the mother had a very significant impact on the education levels of their children and also on the education levels of their grandchildren. The data source, the Spanish Socio Demographic Survey of 1991 (SSS), did not allow us to identify the role of the father in this process. We know that the marriage market in historical Spain was very homogamic and a normal outcome of this fact is that and educated women married educated men. But in historical Spain the gender roles of men and women were very clearly identified and while the role of men was considered to be breadwinning, the primary role of the women was the social and demographic reproduction of the household. Therefore we are assuming here that the education levels of mothers (more than the education levels of the fathers) affected the education of the children since they were the responsible persons for rearing and bearing them and also for their education as a complement of school. Of course we imply here that recent developments of household work distribution between husband and wife that begin to share all experiences from both of the two big sources of work of the household, production (paid labor for an income) and reproduction (rearing and educating children) did not apply to the past. This is an empirical result we obtain from all censuses or demographic lists available.

Another of the very important result by Baizan and Camps (2006) is that the most significant variable explaining fertility levels was the education of the mother. According to the coefficients and levels of statistical significance, this variable is more important than commonly used economic variables used by the literature, such as the difference between urban and rural sectors of employment. SSS does not provide information on religious beliefs which have been identified by Dreze and Sen and Sen as a very important information to explain women's activity both in economic production and demographic reproduction. But during most of the period considered in this essay Spain was under a National Catholic political regime and most of the people were practicing Catholicism the same as in Latin America.

From results obtained in the Spanish case we can conclude that fertility and the education of the children are endogenous to the education levels of the mother:

$$Fi = f(Hmi) \tag{6.1}$$

and

$$Hi = f(Hmi) \tag{6.2}$$

where Fi are the Fertility levels at year i; Hi are the number of years spent at school by children at year i; and Hmi are the education levels of mothers at year i.

We can also express economic growth as a function of production factors, human capital accumulation and the rate of demographic growth. In the aforementioned context of backwardness and in order to simplify the model, we also assume that mortality conditions don't improve and therefore demographic growth is a function only of fertility levels evolution even if this hypotheses, as we will see, does not apply to the developing world of the twentieth century.

$$Yi = f(Ki, Li, Ti, Hi, Pi) \tag{6.3}$$

where levels of per capita GDP (Yi) are a function of levels of industrial capital (Ki), labor (Li), land (Ti), human capital (Hi) and demographic growth (Pi). Since in order to simplify the model we assume that demographic growth only depends on fertility levels, growth of the labor force depends on growth of fertility levels:

$$Pi = Fi \tag{6.4}$$

i

$$Li = Lo\ (1 + Fi) \tag{6.5}$$

From what we have assumed at (6.1), (6.2), (6.4) and (6.5) we can reformulate (6.3) as follows:

$$Yi = f(Ki, Hmi, Lo, To); \tag{6.6}$$

where Lo (labor in the starting point) and To (land) are constants.

Therefore we assume in the model born from the Spanish experience that levels of growth of per capita GDP finally depend on the levels of growth of industrial capital and levels of growth of the education adult women while labor and land are constant.

The Data

Conclusions for Spain come from the Socio Demographic Survey of 1991 and data on female real wages and fertility have been published in by Camps (1995), Llonch (2004), and Cabré (1999). The data used for the international comparisons have been taken from several data sources. Data on women's and children's work, infant mortality and life expectancies can be found in World Bank datasets. Data on females income, gender gap and women empowerment come from United Nations (2005): *Human Development Report*. Data on religious beliefs and ethnic diversity come from the dataset on economic fractionalization by Alesina et al. (2003). Data on income inequality come from Klaus Deininger and Lyn Squire (1996): "A New Data Set Measuring Income Inequality", *World Bank Economic Review*, 10: 3. Data on per capita GDP come from the World Penn Tables and data on education from Barro and Lee.

The Historical Evidence from Catalonia as a Spanish Case Study

During the first third of the twentieth century, and contemporary to the diffusion of the second industrial revolution, physical and human capital shocks sharply transformed Catalan family economies. Between 1860 and 1930 the literacy rates of Catalan population rose from 24 to 82% and the educational gender gap (calculated as the difference between illiteracy of women and men) diminished from 28 to 12% among the same dates. Together with this set of events women's real wages in the textile mills more than doubled in the same period (see Fig. 6.1).

According to Montserrat Llonch (2004) women's human capital was acquired in trade schools (Escola Industrial) that offered vocational training specially adapted to the Catalan textile mills, which moved from town to the countryside using the free energy of water and avoiding labor conflicts caused by anarchist trade unions. Between 1920 and 1930 women's hourly wages increased by an absolute percentage of 70%. The sharp increase in the price of women's time (real wage) increased the opportunity cost of time devoted to unpaid household demands for labor. This had as a consequence the sharp reduction of fertility which attained its minimum of 1.9 (below replacement) as soon as in the years 1930s (legitimate fertility of women of the birth cohort 1910–1914; Cabré 1999)—see Fig. 6.1. The improvement of the education of mothers as we have exposed following the model by Baizan and Camps (2006) was an engine improving the education levels of the children. But this was not the single effect. The important improvement of women's real wages gave the family some of the financial bases to remove children from the labor force. As we stated above it allowed children to postpone the age of entrance to the labor market from 7 to 12.

Therefore in the Catalan case we can clearly identify the effect of the mother's education levels on children's work, education, and fertility and therefore on human capital formation. What is not so clear is the role of this education on improvements on economic growth. According to all estimations Spanish economy only began to grow with vibrancy after 1960. The main reason that explains why Spain did not significantly grow before is the social conflicts of this period.

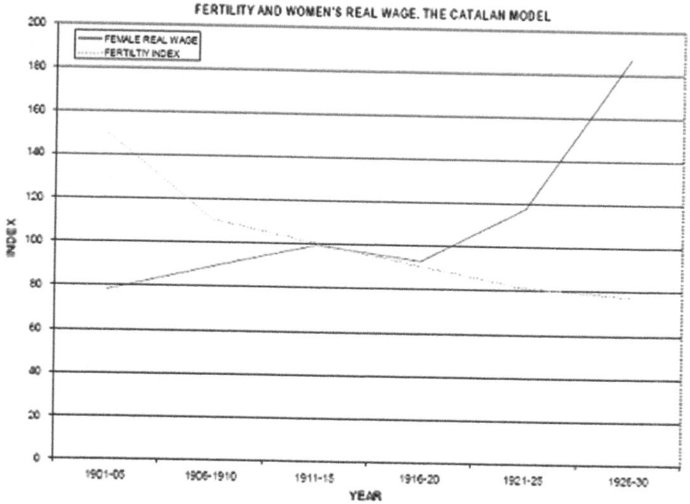

Fig. 6.1 Women's real wages and fertility evolution: the Catalan case, 1900–1935

The opposite and conflicting interests between land owners and owners in general, the clergy and religious institutions, old policy makers and the army among others social groups and the new enlighten and educated working class, liberal professions, new educative institutions brought by the republican governments and new republican politicians caused an armed confrontation during the years of the civil war (1936–1939) that was responsible for negative rates of growth of per capita GDP and was followed by a decade of economic autarchy and virtual economic isolation. Therefore social tensions and political confrontation in the years 1936–1939 till the years 1960s caused a draught back in economic growth measured by per capita GDP (Prados de la Escosura and Rosés 2009). In spite of the achievements attained in the fields of human capital and fertility evolution other historical factors did not allow Spain to grow according to the human capital transformation that the country was experiencing.

Human Capital and Children's Work in Current Developing Countries

One of the most positive consequences of the second globalization era in the years from 1970s to the present has been the improvement of the human capital stock of poor countries, particularly in countries of Latin America and South and East Asia (see Camps and Engerman 2014). Many authors committed with world's economic development have been dealing with these transformations that are more visible if we search the results in variables that affect the quality of life than in variables related to wealth and income. When we want to grasp on the origins of this current transformation, as opposed to the model we built when we were trying to analyze the lessons from the past in Spain, it is important to stress the fact that during the nineteenth century, and as a result of industrial revolution and the first global era levels of per capita GDP between countries (between countries inequality) began to diverge—see Williamson (2008)—but this trend to diverge at the country level increased during the first part of the twentieth century (Sala-i-Martin 2006). In contrast the second globalization era places us in a new context in which a new trend towards convergence started (Sala-i-Martin 2006). But it is important to stress the fact that some of the outcomes of economic openness during the second globalization era have been affecting more clearly human capital spheres of ordinary people's life including health and life expectancies, infant mortality, scientific knowledge, educational infrastructure and services, more than levels of wealth and income (Camps and Engerman 2014).

One of the better-explored aspects of these achievements has been the improvement of life expectancies (Becker 2005) and infant mortality (Bloom and Williamson 1998). In the years 1960–2000 in many poor countries this transformation has been very outstanding and this is the reason why world population has been growing during the last part of the twentieth century. But what we want to stress here are the remaining problems that obscure a positive feedback of human capital accumulation on economic growth (the same as in the micro-historical analysis we made in the first part of the paper).

In current poor countries the same as in the Spanish historical scenarios presented in the first part of the paper we observe that the activity rates of women and children are high, sometimes very high. But it is important to stress that the nature of this labor is very different from what we were trying to describe when we analyzed the Spanish (Catalan) case (Fig. 6.2).

It is possible to report using the time budgets built by the *Human Development Report* (2003) of current poor countries that the number of hours women can allocate to paid production per day is lower or equal than 4 while domestic chores imply a dedication of 6 and 7 hours per day. Housework technologies are very difficult to globalize since they affect family formation patterns which in turn can be partly explained by social capital variables such as religion and culture. In many countries of Africa, Latin America, and South Asia competing demands of women's time for paid and unpaid work do not allow them to fully develop their human capital capabilities and those of their children. The very different nature of women's work in poor countries has further implications, because in this case their paid activity is positively correlated with infant mortality and illness. In turn these poor countries where women and children are still working in the informal sector of

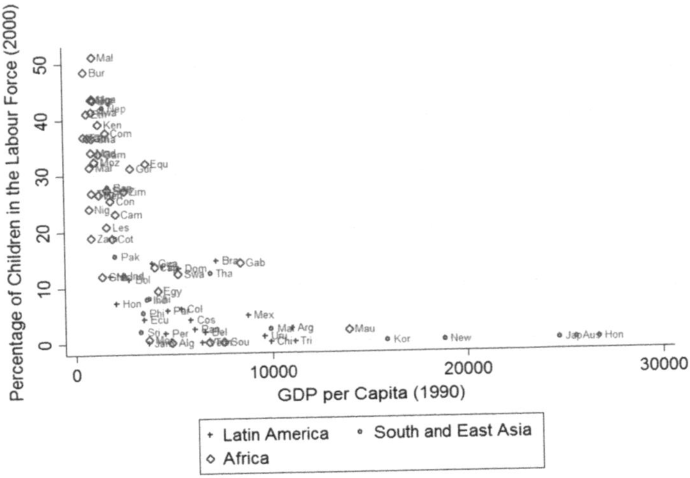

Fig. 6.2 Child labour and GDP per capita in the developing world

the economy are the countries showing higher levels of within the country inequality of income distribution (Figs. 6.3, 6.4, 6.5, and 6.6).

In Fig. 6.7, we plot the Gini coefficients of income distribution by Deininger and Squire (1996) data for years 1990–1995 and its relation with the gender gap and we obtain a slight negative correlation. The effect of the Ginis of income inequality of the economy on the gender gap is nearly constant. On the other hand the relationship between Gini and children's participation in the labor force is positive and if we exclude countries where children don't work is U shaped. Children's work is more intense in very unequal countries and in countries that are too poor to exhibit very high Ginis. Several authors have stressed that economic inequality achieve lower values in open economies and in countries where women are more visible in public and professional decision making (women empowerment). All these events occur more easily in egalitarian societies than in extremely unequal ones were most women have low access to human capital services for them and also for their children (Fig. 6.8).

The results from the regression analysis are consistent with the model we made explicit in Part 2 of the paper. In Table 6.1, we see that

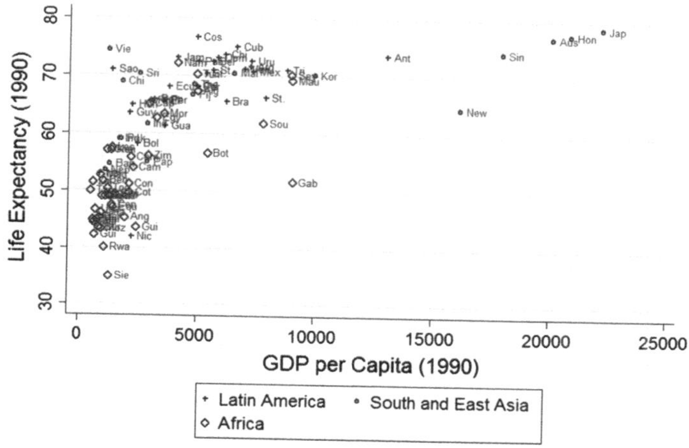

Fig. 6.3 Life expectancy and GDP, developing world

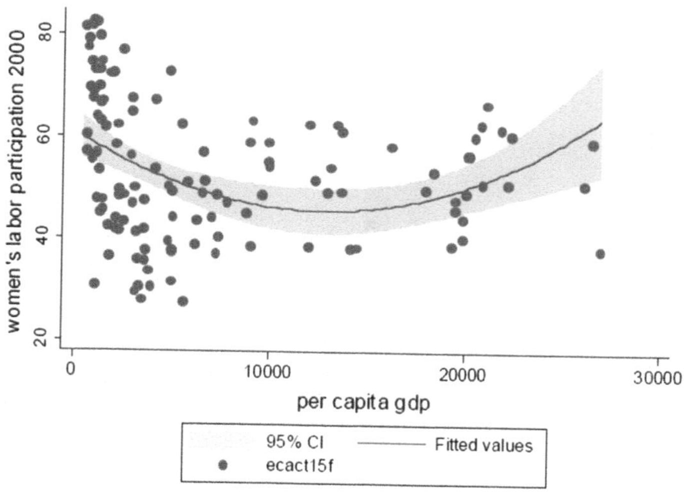

Fig. 6.4 The U shaped female labor participation function in development. World wide sample, 2000

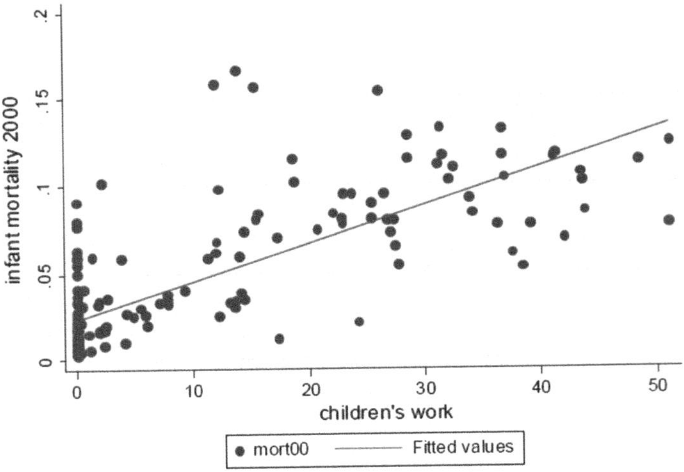

Fig. 6.5 The influence of children's work on infant mortality. World wide sample, 2000

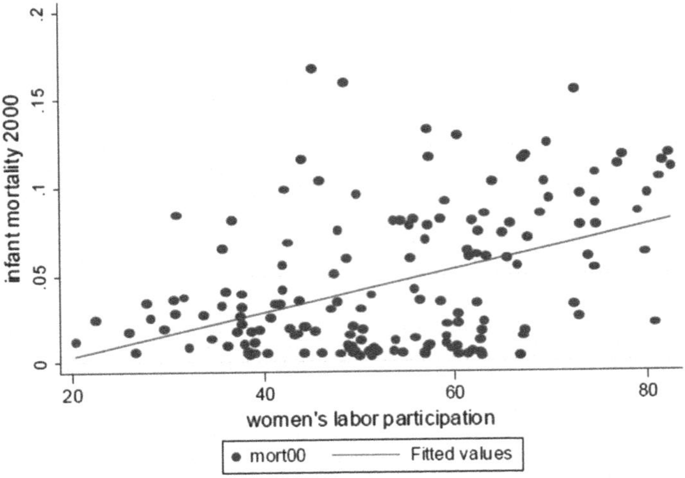

Fig. 6.6 The influence of female labor participation in infant mortality. World wide sample, 2000

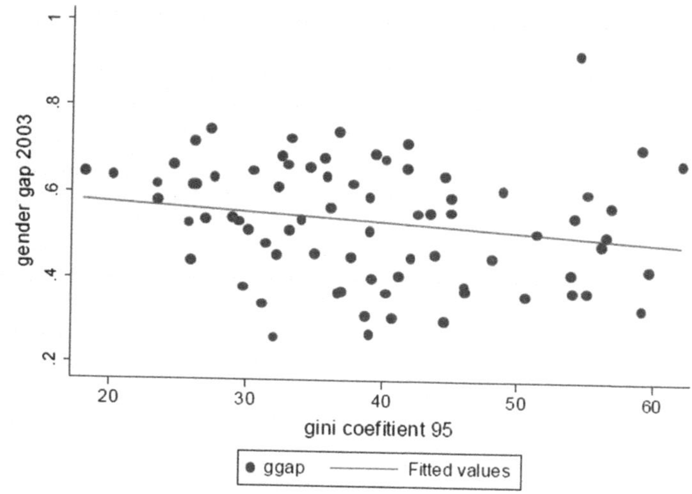

Fig. 6.7 The relationship between the gender gap (income female/income male) and economic inequality

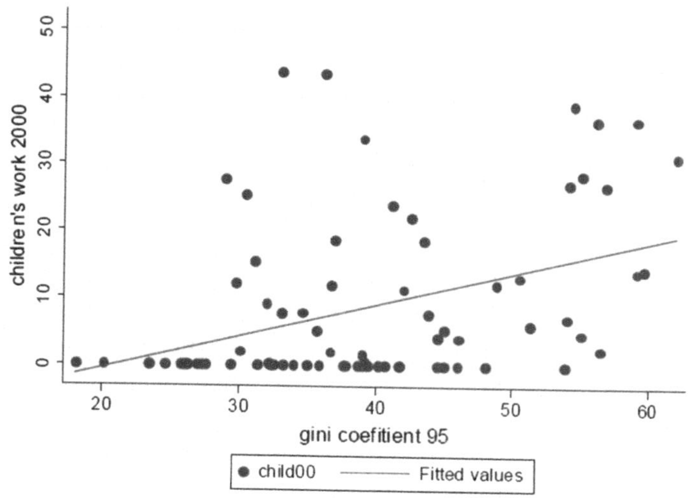

Fig. 6.8 The relationship between children's work and economic inequality

Table 6.1 Explaining children's work in nowadays developing countries. An across country panel linear regression, 1960–2000

Dependent variable: Percentage of children aged 10–14 in the labor force	
Log per capita GDP	−0.273 (0.231)
Years in school women/men	−0.740 (0.007)***
Years in school women	−0.885 (0.152)***
Mother's mortality at birth	−0.001 (0.0002)***
Fertility	1.257 (0.166)***
Constant	18.638 (2.973)***

Standard error in brackets; *$p<0.1$, **$p<0.05$, ***$p<0.01$
$N=833$; $R^2=0.7194$ (within: 0.4985, between: 0.7365)
Wald χ^2 (5) = 849.25

children's work continues to exist in extremely gendered societies where the human capital of women is very low in absolute and in relative (to men) terms, and fertility levels are high. In Table 6.1, we can see that the intensity of children's work is negatively correlated with the human capital of women and this variable (also human capital of women/human capital of men) has a high coefficient and a statistically significant result. On the other hand the sign of the coefficient of fertility is positive and this fact implies that the countries with the highest size of the offspring in average terms are also those exhibiting highest rates of children's work. According to Table 6.2 this has further implications on economic growth. The rate of participation of children in the labor force has negative effects on the level of per capita GDP while religious beliefs have a much lower impact on economic growth than the gender bias.

In a comparative framework the poorest countries from Africa are those with more severe mortality conditions, highest fertility levels (Camps and Engerman 2014) and also highest income inequality and gender gap. But notice also that the levels of the gender gap are high in some of the Latin American countries in contrast with countries of South and East Asia. We also see in Fig. 6.3 that Latin America is a continent with high variance in life expectancies, with results between

Table 6.2 The influence of social capital in per capita GDP

Dependent variable	Whole sample log (GDP per capita)	Developing	S/E Asia/LA
Percentage of children labor	−0.049	−0.035	−0.03
	(0.005)***	(0.005)***	(0.024)
Measure for openness	3.437	0.281	2.378
	(0.917)***	(1.445)	(3.161)
Catholic	0.002	0.012	0.003
	(0.003)	(0.004)***	(0.006)
Other Christian	0.007	0.016	0.031
	(0.004)*	(0.008)**	(0.019)
Muslim	−0.003	0.007	0.00
	(0.003)	(0.004)*	(0.007)
Jewish	0.758	−0.131	0.208
	(0.199)***	(0.580)	(0.883)
Hindu	0.005	0.025	0.00
	(0.009)	(0.009)***	(0.036)
Buddhist	0.013	0.016	0.015
	(0.005)**	(0.005)***	(0.008)*
Measure for political instability	−0.819	−0.395	−1.167
	(0.233)***	(0.271)	(0.663)*
Women in gov. (%)	0.01	−0.008	0.001
	(0.006)*	(0.009)	(0.002)
Constant	7.482	7.227	7.43
	(0.341)***	(0.369)***	(0.767)***
Observations	68	46	26
R^2	0.85	0.79	0.65

Standard errors in brackets
$^{*}p<0.1$, $^{**}p<0.05$, $^{***}p<0.01$

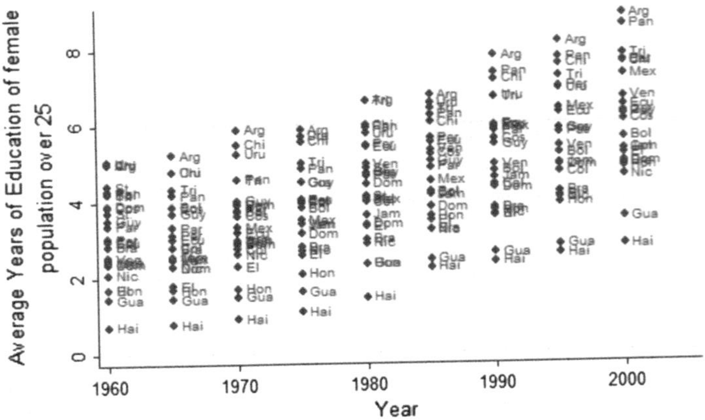

Fig. 6.9 Years of schooling on adult women in the biggest countries of Latin America (1960–2000)

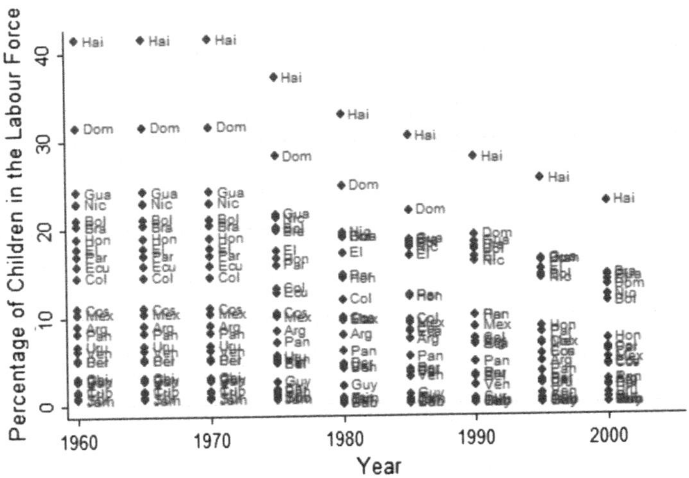

Fig. 6.10 Child labor force participation in the biggest countries of Latin America (1960–2000)

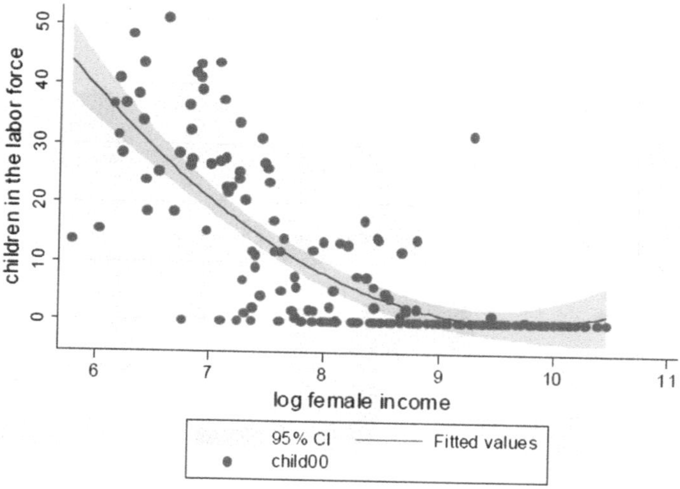

Fig. 6.11 Children's work as a function of women's earnings. World wide sample, 2000–2003

50 and 75 years at the end of the twentieth century. But in richer countries where the gender bias is low and the participation of children in the labor force is also low both infant mortality and life expectancies have improved. In Figs. 6.9 and 6.10, we present the evolution of female years of schooling and children participation levels in the labor force in Latin American countries in the period 1960–2000. Notice the trend of female years of education to increase and the trend of children levels of labor participation to decrease in all countries. Therefore the human capital century has also reached Latin American countries and better levels of education both for men and women have implied the improvement of living conditions. On the other hand these achievements, specially the removal of children from the labor force have stimulated economic growth by means of the improvement of education levels (Reimers 2006). But the same as in the Spanish case other economic factors have fostered low levels of economic achievement. After the ISI period, during the 1980s the foreign debt payments problems implied serious adjustment measures that sacrificed levels of consumption and investment and economic development in some of the Latin American countries (Figs. 6.11 and 6.12).

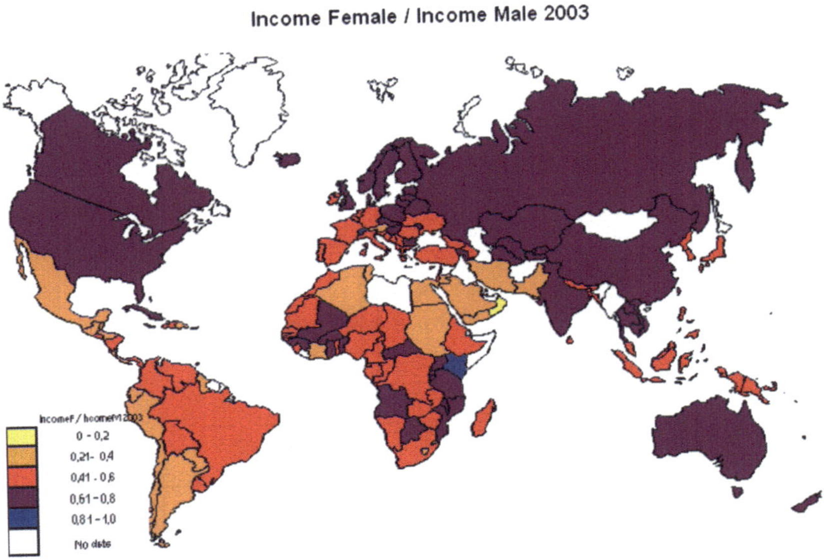

Fig. 6.12 The gender gap. World countries, 2003

Conclusion

The twentieth century has significantly been labeled as the human capital century. In this paper we have reported some key features of human capital in developing countries and more specifically in Latin America by focusing on key aspects of women and children labor market participation levels in a comparative framework. While in Catalonia and parts of Spain the increase of the levels of education of women and children was a process that began in the nineteenth century and took place during the twentieth century, in developing countries and more precisely in Latin America the process of educational reform was slow and began in the twentieth century (Reimers 2006). Uneducated mothers with low levels of income conceived uneducated children that were soon part of the labor force. During the twentieth century this process has a higher intensity in the poorest countries of the world that exhibit high female and child participation levels in unskilled occupations of the informal sector of the economy. But at least in the Latin American case we have proved the trend towards the improvement of women's and children's laboring condition during the recent past. The increase of levels of education of women brought with it the decline of levels of participation by children and the improvement of demographic conditions ([infant mortality and fertility] Camps and Engerman 2014). This has further implications for the acceleration of economic growth in the twenty-first century but this is not part of our history.

Acknowledgements This article was supported by the Ministry of Science and Technology, project HAR 2012-3952-CO-01 and a Barcelona Graduate School of Economics Seed Grant.

Bibliography

Alesina, A., Devleeschauwer, A., Easterly, W., Kurlat, S., Waczirag, R., "Fractionalization", *Journal of Economic Growth*, VIII (2003): 155–194.

Baizan, P., Camps, E., "The Impact of Women's Educational and Economic Resources on Fertility. Spanish Birth Cohorts 1901–1950", in *Were Women Present at the Demographic Transition?*, edited by A. Janssens. Bern, Peter Lang, 2006.

Barro, R., Lee, W., "A New Data Set of Educational Attainment in the World, 1950–2010", *Journal of Development Economics*, 104C (2013): 184–198.

Barro, R., Sala-i-Martin, X., *Economic Growth*. Cambridge, MA, MIT Press, 2003.

Bass, L.E., *Child Labor in Sub-Saharan Africa*. London, Lynne Rienner, 2004.

Basu, K., "The Intriguing Relation Between Adult Minimum Wage and Child Labour", *The Economic Journal*, 110 (2000): 462.

Basu, K., Hoang Van, P., "The Economics of Child Labor", *The American Economics Review*, 88 (1998): 3–5.

Becker, G., *Human Capital*. Chicago, University of Chicago Press, 1993.

Becker, G., "Quantity and Quality of Life and World Inequality", *The American Economic Review*, 95 (2005):1.

Bloom, D., Williamson, J.G., "Demographic Transitions and Economic Miracles in Emerging Asia", *World Bank Economic Review*, 12, no. 3 (September 1998): 419–455.

Cabré, A., *Els sistema català de reproducció*. Barcelona, Pòrtic, 1999.

Caldwell, J.C., *Theory of Fertility Decline*. New York, Academic Press, 1982.
Camps, E., *La formación del Mercado de trabajo en la Cataluña industrial en el siglo XIX*. Madrid, Ministerio de Trabajo y Seguridad Social, Colección de Historia Social, 1995.
Camps, E., "The Rise and Decline of Children's Labor Participation Levels During the Early Stages of Industrialization. Catalonia (1850–1925)", in *Child's Labor Global Past*, edited by K. Lietten and E. Van Nederven Meerk. New York, Peter Lang, 2011.
Camps, E., Engerman, S., "World Population Growth: The Force of Recent Historical Trends", *Journal of Interdisciplinary History*, 44, no. 4 (2014): 509–526.
Cocharne, S. H., *Education and Fertility: What Do We Really Know?* Baltimore, World Bank, 1979.
Cunningham, H., Viazzo, P.P. "Child Labor in Historical Perspective, 1800–1995. Case Studies from Europe and North America Since 1830", *Economic History Review*, LIII, no. 3 (1996).
Deininger, K., Squire, L., "A News Data Set Measuring Income Inequality", *World Bank Economic Review*, 10 (1996): 3.
Desai, S., "Children at Risk: The Role of Family Structure in Latin America and West Africa", *Population and Development Review*, 18 (1992): 4.
Galor, O., Weil, D.N., "The Gender Gap, Fertility and Growth", *The American Economic Review*, 86, nos. 3–5 (1996): 374–387.
García-Balañá, A., *La fabricació de la fàbrica. Treball i política a la Catalunya cotonera (1784–1874)*. Barcelona, Publicacions de l'Abadia de Montserrat, 2004.
Goldin, C., *Understanding the Gender Gap*. Oxford, Oxford University Press, 1990.
Goldin C., "The U Shaped Female Labor Force Function in Economic Development and Economic History", NBER Working Paper Series No. 4707, 1994.
Goldin, C., Katz, L., *The Race Between Education and Technology*. Cambridge, MA, Harvard University Press, 2008.
Lindert, P.H., Williamson, J.G., "Does Globalization Make the World More Unequal?", in *Globalization in Historical Perspective*, edited by M. Bordo et al. Chicago and London, NBER and The University of Chicago Press, 2003.
Llonch, M., "Jornada, salarios y costes laborales en el sector textil catalán (1891–1936)", *Revista de Historia Industrial*, 26 (2004): 101–140.

Prados de la Escosura, L., Rosés, J.R., "Human Capital and Economic Growth in Spain, 1850–2000", Working Papers in Economic History, Universidad Carlos III, 2009.

Reimers, F., "Education and Social Progress", in *The Cambridge Economic History Latin America*, vol. II, edited by V. Blumer-Thomas et al. New York, Cambridge University Press, 2006.

Sala-i-Martin, X., "The World Distribution of Income: Falling Poverty and... Convergence Period", *Quarterly Journal of Economics*, 121, no. 2 (May 2006): 351–397.

Sen, A., "More Than 100 Million of Women Are Missing", *The New York Review*, December 20, 1990.

United Nations, *Human Development Report*. New York, Oxford University Press, 2005.

Williamson, J.G., *Coping with City Growth*. Oxford, Oxford University Press, 1990.

Williamson, J.G., "Globalization and Inequality, Past and Present", *World Bank Research Observer*, 12 (1997): 117–135.

Williamson, J.G., "Globalization and the Great Divergence: Terms of Trade, Booms, Volatility and the Poor Periphery, 1782–1913", *European Review of Economic History*, 12, no. 3 (December 2008): 355–391.

7

Education, Gender Gap, and Market Openness: A Comparative Study of Urban Latin America and East Asia (1970–2000)

Abstract In this paper we present: (1) The available data on comparative gender inequality at the macroeconomic level and (2) Gender inequality measures at the microeconomic and case study level. We see that market openness has a significant effect on the narrowing of the human capital gender gap. Globalization and market openness stand as factors that improve both the human capital endowments of women and their economic position. But we also see that the effects of culture and religious beliefs are very different. While Catholicism has a statistically significant influence on the improvement of the human capital gender gap, Muslim and Buddhist religious beliefs have the opposite effect and increase human capital gender differences. In the second global era, some Catholic Latin American countries benefited from market openness in terms of the human capital and income gender gap, whereas we find the opposite impact in Buddhist and Muslim countries like China and South Korea where women's economic position has worsened in terms of human capital and wage inequality.

E. Camps-Cura, *Changes in Population, Inequality and Human Capital Formation in the Americas in the Nineteenth and Twentieth Centuries*, Palgrave Studies in Economic History,
https://doi.org/10.1007/978-3-030-21351-0_7

Keywords Gender gap · Market openness · Christian · Religion · Culture

Introduction

In last few years, a considerable amount of literature on economic inequality, its connection to globalization, and its influence on economic growth has been published. A large school of economic historians, Jeffrey G. Williamson, Peter Lindert and many of their co-authors, friends, and students, have been dealing with this topic although they have not concentrated on the topic of gender. This literature has shown changes in the relative prices of production factors during the first global era (1820–1913) that imply changes in long term total income inequality distribution (Lindert and Williamson 2003), which were driven by labor supply forces and fostered convergence of the economies involved (O'Rourke and Williamson 1999). But it is much more difficult to frame general conclusions on income inequality during the second globalization era, in which the intensity of migration flow and capital movement is lower than in the first, while trade liberalization policies are more widespread. According to some perspectives, this is a critical factor of the second globalization era because Latin American countries, with a long tradition in protectionist trade policies, had to pay the price of adjusting to free trade and this normally implied the curtail of public and social spending and subsidies (such as public schools and public health), which particularly affect women and children, and ultimately the formation of human capital (see on the topic Thorp 1998).

In most of the empirical results regarding the second globalization era, the unit of analysis of the datasets is the household, and the results refer to Gini coefficients for income or expenditure (see, for instance, Deininger and Squire 1996, 1998; World Bank 1995; Chai and Chai 1994; Higgins and Williamson 2003; Riskin et al. 2001). Other innovative approaches have focused on individuals instead of households, using national income shares and national account information (see Bourguignon and Morrison 2002; Sala-i-Martin 2003), and have raised new conclusions on the reasons behind the diminution of worldwide global inequality and global poverty rates during the last quarter of the twentieth century. The impact of economic liberalization of the most populated countries of the world, China and India, is the key factor.

In this essay we want to go a step further. We want to explore the implications that changes in the gender gap in developing countries have had on income distribution and gender income distribution during the second globalization era. Therefore our unit of analysis must be the individual and not the household, since Gini coefficients for household income mask important information on the unequal economic position of women inside the household. This means that our measure of inequality is going to be different from conventional household inequality measures. In most countries of the world, marriage is very homogamic and the wealth backgrounds of the bride and groom have a major influence on partner choice in the marriage market and on family and household formation. The implication of this fact is that household measures for inequality normally exaggerate real inequality among people at the average level. Therefore there is a difference in the magnitude of our inequality indicators with respect to the traditional household Gini coefficients. We are going to measure the evolution of wage differences between people (not households) stressing the differences between men and women.

The countries studied here are in Latin America and East Asia. We think that the comparison of Latin American and East Asian experiences is especially worthwhile since income inequality and the gender gap are shaped in significantly different ways on these two continents. According to the standard Gini calculations based on household budgets by Deininger and Squire 1996, Asia has been a more egalitarian continent than Latin America. But as regards the educational gender gap, we obtain an egalitarian distribution in Latin America and more unequal gender patterns in East and South Asia (Barro and Lee 2000). These factors challenge recent research on the role of women's education in the transmission of human capital to the children (Galor and Weil 1996; Hazan and Berdugo 2004). On the other hand, they suggest that the patterns of income distribution in both regions of the world mask different magnitudes of the gender gap originated by economic and cultural factors, as we shall underline later.

A second set of hypotheses refers to the impact of increasing competition in labor markets—brought about by globalization- on the narrowing of gender gap. As stated by the simple Stopler-Samuelson model, free trade has further implications on the rise of wages on the relative abundant production factor in developing countries, unskilled work (Samuelson 1948). Since most unskilled labor is often performed by women, we can infer from the Stopler-Samuelson model that globalization, which causes an increasing demand for women's labor, should have as a final result the relative increase of women's levels of participation and the diminution of the gender gap (see the case of Mexico in Dell 2005; Artecona and Cunningham 2002; Garcia-Cuellar 2001). For the case of Mexico it has been effectively proven that economic integration in NAFTA since 1994 has led to an increase in female participation and a decrease in the gender gap.

On the other hand, according to Becker (1957), gender discrimination seems to depend on male cultural tastes and it is eliminated by the increasing intensity of competitive market forces. According to recent research, economic competition brought about by economic openness and equal treatment laws result in a considerable narrowing of the gender gap (see Weichselbaumer and Winter-Ebmer 2003).

In this paper, we analyze the impact of the globalization process and religious beliefs on human capital formation and the gender gap in these two different cultural settings. First, by means of regression analysis we study the cultural and market openness determinants of the human capital gender gap in East Asian and Latin American countries. Second, we have reconstructed the gendered inequality indexes for a sample of East Asian and Latin American countries. In this part of the paper we want to frame explanations on the evolution of the gender gap and its impact on inequality. We think that, in this respect, our results are new since we have found very few studies that take into account including women's earnings in the calculation of income inequality indexes. The countries chosen are China, South Korea, and Singapore in Asia, and Argentina, Uruguay, and Brasil in Latin America. The available information is still preliminary, but we think our evidence is a step forward in the research of the relationship between globalization and the gender gap.

The Data

It is well known that when we include women's income information in world's international comparisons the first problem we have is the lack of reliable data. In poor countries part of the work performed by women is in the informal economy, performed at home and for piece rates. The available information on this kind of work is still scattered in few datasets and not comparable across countries. The same problems arise to evaluate women's income derived from properties and other financial assets. This lack of information makes the comparison of women and men's incomes very difficult, almost impossible.

This is why we have limited our observations to urban wage earnings. As we shall see different sources report female and male wage earnings in a very systematic way, although this analysis also has some limitations. Income inequality measures are higher than wage inequality indexes, since wage earnings show a lower dispersion than total incomes. Additionally, poor people, workers in the informal sector of the economy, employers, and property owners are excluded from our analysis, which means that our data is not useful to analyze some economy-wide changes. But instead our data allows us to analyze rigorously and systematically gender differences in wage earnings, the main engines causing them and their implications for income inequality evolution.

In Part 4 of this paper we present the world results on the earnings gender gap on the bases of UN datasets. UN uses them to calculate Gender Development Index and the Gender Empowerment Index. These data are available in the Human Development Report (2005). It is important to stress here that UN data referring to female incomes and the ratio female/male incomes are different from the data we use to compute inequality in Part 5 of the paper. To estimate gender differences in earnings as can be observed in Map 7.1 the UN uses the ratio of the female non agricultural wage over the male non agricultural wage, the female and male shares of the economically active population, the total female and male population, and per capita GDP(PPP US$). When data on gender wages are not available, the UN assumes a rate of 75% in female/male wages outside the agriculture. This is certainly

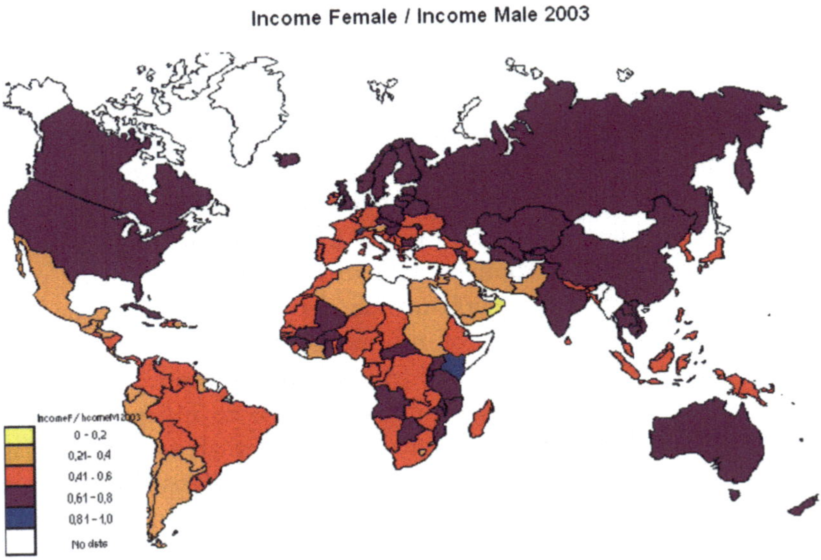

Map 7.1 The earnings gender gap at the world level, 2003 (*Source* UN 2005)

a limitation of this source. In Map 7.1 we use this data because they are the first available that make possible worldwide comparisons. But we are aware of the deficits of this data, particularly when we compare our results on the wage gender gap with the UN indicator of income gender gap. Nonetheless, we think it is worth to make use of the first evidence available on gender income differences in order to make the first comparative analysis.

In the last part of the paper we estimate the inequality indexes and gendered inequality indexes of urban wage workers for a sample of six countries of Asia and Latin America: Brasil, Argentina, and Uruguay (1975–1995) in Latin America and China, Korea, and Singapore (1985–1995) in South East Asia. It is important to stress that the measure of inequality we obtain in Part 5 is different from the approach presented in Map 7.1 on the bases of the data provided by UN. The Gini and Theil indexes presented in the last part of the paper give an indication on the unitary basic wage dispersion controlled by gender. Therefore aspects that are crucial to represent gender inequality by

UN (like PPP GNP, employment of women, or the female/male rate of population) and that may give broad hints on earnings differentials of women/men may hide other dynamic aspects such as human capital provision or the influence of culture on well-being (and not merely on incomes).

For the Asian cases of China, South Korea, and Singapore the data source is the October Inquiry (OI). OI is an annual survey conducted by ILO since the mid-twentieth century. The Inquiry collects returns on wages by occupation in October every year as reported by the Statistical Institutes of different national governments. The number of countries and the scope of information it covers has enlarged and improved over time. Since 1983, the survey includes 140 wage categories for very thin and well-specified occupations. In some cases specific information is missing, in which case ILO fills it in by using average wages. Other problems arise from this source when you want to make the information comparable. Wages can be expressed hourly, daily, weekly, or monthly with very few scattered information on the number of working hours per day or per week according to the country. All these problems are being analyzed by R. Oostendrop and R. Freeman who are calibrating the data to make feasible international comparisons.

In the countries we have chosen the wage rate information refers always to monthly earnings and the male and female earnings are specified in all the occupations. In fact, from all the countries for which the survey gives information these 3 countries are the most reliable in terms of data source. These wage rates refer to net earnings of the basic wage and do not include earnings derived from productivity plusses or extraordinary working hours or days. Therefore the observations from our sample once standardized are homogeneous and allow for international comparisons.

To calculate the inequality indexes we have matched the gendered wage rates by occupation as specified by OI with the gender employment of the census returns according to ISCO ILO classification criteria. Wage and employment information do not always have a single match, and our criteria has been to maximize employment and to calculate average wages per employment category. The census employment categories that do not have any match with OI wage information are ignored. Since most of the wage information refers to the economy of urban areas the final employment categories derived from this matching process belong to the industrial and services sectors and can be considered representative of the urban setting. In the case of China OI makes explicit that the wage information is urban. South Korea and Singapore are highly urbanized countries and OI gives very little information on rural agrarian wages.

Data on gender wage earnings for the cases of Argentina, Uruguay, and Brasil come from the Household Surveys of every country. These surveys are normally used to analyze household income inequality, but they also provide information on wage earnings of individual members of the household, men and women. For the Latin American case this information is increasingly available since the 1970s and can be regarded as a rich reservoir of data for the analysis of living standards and income distribution. Household Surveys inquire on the basic wage weekly or monthly. In the cases of Argentina, Uruguay, and Brasil and in order to make possible the comparisons with the Asian data we have only selected the urban data, in the case of Argentina more specifically Gran Buenos Aires.

The Methodology

In Part 4, we present a panel regression analysis on the human capital gender gap, 1960–2000 trying to test the significance of culture and market openness on the gender gap. In Part 5, we have calculated the Gini index for earnings inequality in the economy as a whole as well as for inequality within men and within women. But since the Gini index for a population is not a linear function of the Gini indexes of its subgroups if these subgroups overlap in the earnings distribution, as it happens in the case of gender, we cannot decompose the relative contribution of gender inequality to inequality in the economy using Gini. The alternatives are the so-called generalized entropy measures, of which the best known are the Theil indexes. These indexes, while keeping the same properties as the Gini index, allow estimation of how much inequality is explained by inequality within groups and how much by inequality between groups. We use these indexes to decompose inequality into its gendered sources. More specifically, this paper uses the so-called Theil's L index or mean log deviation measure, the most commonly used in the literature. Its formula can be expressed as follow:

$$I_0 = \frac{1}{N}\sum_{i=1}^{n} \ln \frac{\bar{y}}{y_i}$$

where I_0 is the inequality index, N is the total size of the population, and y is income or earnings. One of the properties of these indicators, as already said, is that they can be decomposed as a function of some subgroups characteristics. Subgroups can be defined according to occupation, age, or gender, among others. Let y_k be the average income of a subgroup, n_k the population in the subgroup, and I_0 the inequality index for the subgroup, then,

$$I_0 = \sum_{k=1}^{n} \left(\frac{n_k}{N}\right) I_0^k + \sum_{k=1}^{n} \frac{n_k}{N} \ln \frac{1}{y_k/\bar{Y}}$$

The first term represents within-group inequality, and the second term between-group inequality. We will use this to assess how earnings inequality within and across gender contributes to inequality in the economy. Within-gender inequality refers to the diversity of male wages and female wages. If over time wages become less spread out in one of the subgroups, women for example, this would contribute to reduce inequality in the economy, other things equal. The second term, between-gender inequality, refers to inequality between subgroups, that is, it ignores the spectrum of wages within each subgroup and looks at differences in average wages across subgroups. In other words, it measures the contribution of the gender gap to overall inequality. If women's average earnings increase, for example—and taking into account that women are the lowest paid subgroup—inequality will decrease, ceteris paribus.

Another indicator of gender inequality is occupational segregation, that is, the tendency for men and women to be employed in different occupations. High levels of segregation have been considered to be a significant factor in the discrepancy between the wages of women and men, and generally to be at the root of gender inequalities. In order to measure segregation, the most common indicator is the dissimilarity index, which generally measures whether a particular group is distributed across occupations in the same way as another group. The formula to calculate gender occupational segregation is the following:

$$S = \frac{1}{2}\sum_i |m_i - f_i|$$

where m_i and f_i are the percentage of male and female employment in occupation *i*. The dissimilarity index is a measure from 0 to 1. The closer to 1 the values, the more segregated the two groups are.

Real Income Versus Human Capital Gender GAP

Since the classical book by Ester Boserup (1970) many authors have insisted on the importance that all factors fostering female market power have in the erosion of the gender gap. Human capital and exposure to the labor market are some of these factors. Institutional and cultural factors promoting more bargaining power by women are other elements (Field 2003, 2005). But in several poor countries of Asia and Latin America women may have problems to develop market power. One of their main restrictions refers to available time to devote to market activities. In Table 7.1, we present the working time balance on men and women in several countries of Latin America and Asia. This table is based on scattered data at the country level, and must be analyzed with caution. But as a general remark Table 7.1 shows that in poor countries women work more hours than men because of the loads of work in non-market activities. With the available technologies for domestic work, in poor countries women must deploy between 5.5 and 6 hours daily to unpaid work. Part of this work is addressed to supply goods and services that in rich countries are offered by the market. This is an important time restriction when considering the possibilities of women's market exposure in poor countries. This situation of time collapse between alternative activities only gradually changes as a consequence of

Table 7.1 The use of work time according to gender in poor countries, 1990–2000 (unweighted averages)

Total work time	Urban areas		Rural areas	
	Hours/day	%	Hours/day	%
Women	8.01		10.28	
Market activities	2.48	31	3.6	38
Non-market activities	5.52	69	6.03	62
Men	7.55		8.58	
Market activities	5.96	79	6.52	76
Non-market activities	1.58	21	2.05	24
Women/men (%)	107		120	

Source: *Human Development Report* (2005, calculated from Table 29, p. 315). Based on time surveys. Urban areas based in Colombia, Indonesia, Kenya, Nepal, Venezuela. Rural areas based in Bangladesh, Guatemala, Kenya, Nepal, Philippines

human capital investments and improvements, which increase women's capabilities and market dexterity and as a result the value of their market activities also improves.

A first problem we face when we deal with the gender gap is that we must make explicit what we want to measure since several variables account for gender differences. The most widespread meaning of the gender gap is the wage gender differential of women relative to men. This in turn implies that in a given society exists equality of opportunities and freedom of choice. In historical terms the emancipation of women and their massive incorporation into the labor markets dates from World War II in the capitalist World, and from the soviet revolution in the communist world.

In this second case while employment is universal both for men and women freedom of choice is very limited. Anyway, and in spite the failure of communism and socialism as a path of economic development since the 1990s, in Map 7.1, we can see that countries like China, India, or Russia stand among the most egalitarian in terms of income gender gap, together with the United States, Canada, Australia, and New Zealand. Indeed Map 7.1 is also clear to show that the income gender gap has a lot to do with economic inequality in general. Being the most unequal regions of the world, countries of Latin America, Africa, and the Middle East are also the countries that exhibit the highest wage gender gap. We must put special stress to socialist countries in transition because in this case economic inequality is increasing sharply in the recent past while the tradition of women to work for a wage still remains, and the income gender gap is lower.

But if these are the results we obtain from wage and earning rates, can we assert that these indexes measure the real gender gap? Amartya Sen (1990, 1992, 2003) has been the lider author stressing the connections between market exposure and cultural backgrounds and the real gender gap. In countries such as China and India many women have to confront social exclusion. In most of these transition economies, the low preferences of men regarding visibility and exposure of women mean a real threat to equality of opportunities according to gender. Economic backwardness but also cultural factors can explain the lack of equity in the supply of human capital services according to gender, both in terms of health and education. This is not only visible in the data of school achievement and attainment by Barro and Lee but also by the computation of missing women by Sen which normally mean that women lose their biological (genetic) advantage and prematurely die.

In Table 7.2, by means of a linear panel across country regression we have compared the effects of globalization and market exposure with those of religion, on the human capital gender gap. The human capital gender gap is calculated as the ratio "years of women enrolment in school/years of men enrolment in school". Market openness has a statistically significant positive role in diminishing the human capital gender gap. Indeed in totally autharquic societies women can only follow the orders of the ruler. In more open societies women have real freedom to choose, and this normally implies that they also have more visibility, exposure, and empowerment and as consequence the human capital gender gap diminishes. If this is the universal role of market openness we can see that the influence of other variables can eliminate the effects of market exposure. In Table 7.2, we show that culture, here measured by means of religious beliefs is not neutral. In Buddhist and Muslim countries religion is a factor that fosters the increase of differences between men and women and enlarges the human capital gender gap. Instead in catholic countries, such as Latin American counties, Catholicism acts a factor that promotes the diminution of the human

Table 7.2 The role of market openness and culture in shaping the human capital gender gap

Across country linear panel regression, 1960–2000			
Dependent variable: years of school women/years of school men			
	(1)	(2)	(3)
Market openness	0.0023139 (0.0012274)*	0.0020139 (0.0012218)*	0.0023931 (0011935)**
Gini coef * urban share	−0.0594599 (0.0315714)*	0.0206303 (0.02791)	0.0494648 (0.028893)*
Catholic * urban share	0.1386253 (0.0421793)***		
Muslim * urban share		−0.2671665 (0.0711539)***	
Buddhist * urban share			−0.2767896 (0.0518004)***
1960	−0.1990823 (0.0288728)***	−0.2109165 (0.0303868)***	−0.2027946 (0.0277031)***
1965	−0.1914564 (0.0279903)***	−0.2053038 (0.0294233)***	−0.1917831 (0.0267985)***
1970	−0.2014801 (0.026537)***	−0.2136894^ (0.0280565)***	−0.1996761 (0.0253638)***
1975	−0.1794736 (0.026617)***	−0.1931434 (0.02813)***	−0.1793117 (0.0254354)***
1980	−0.1490377 (0.0263726)***	−0.1640693 (0.0277864)***	−0.1517645 (0.0252067)***
1985	−0.1257156 (0.0261615)***	−0.1390088 (0.0269203)***	−0.1280971 (0.0249982)***
1990	−0.0979618 (0.0255197)***	−0.112742 (0.0269203)***	−0.102029 (0.0243878)***
1995		−0.0138033 (0.0305774)	
2000	0.0168061 (0.0305567)		0.0135757 (0.0291494)
Constant	0.80335987 (0.0407258)***	0.8630158 (0.0415124)***	0.8199689 (0.0405604)***
Times fixed effects	Yes	Yes	Yes
Country fixed effects	Yes	Yes	Yes
N	328	328	328
	R^2 within = 0.4311	0.4391	0.4933
	Between = 0.0575	0.0671	0.0027
	Overall = 0.0258	0.0637	0.0140
	Wald $\chi^2(11)$ = 190.54	193.22	226.92

Source Data on religion com from Alesina et al., and data on market openness and school attendance from Barro and Lee

*p 10%, **p 5%, ***p 1%

capital gender gap. May be this is the reason why during the last 40 years and together with more market openness, in catholic countries of Latin America there has been sensible achievements in women's human capital investment (or improvement of their health and education backgrounds). This is visible using all sort of variables related to health and education like infant mortality by gender, life expectancies, and school enrolment and achievement according to gender.

To summarize, we can stress the fact that globalization and market exposure have a positive effect in the relative situation of women. This is a factor that helps to develop more capabilities and to make effective individual choices, as we have shown in Table 7.2. This fact has as a consequence the diminution of the differences in human capital endowments of men and women. But the net impact of globalization on gender differences depends a lot on the cultural and religious background of every country. While in Latin American Catholic countries women benefited from more market freedom and improved their human capital endowments relative to men, in countries of East Asia like China and South Korea, prevalent religious practices like Buddhist and Muslim beliefs have had as an outcome the worsening of female human capital investments, both in terms of health and education.

A Micro Analysis of the Gendered Wage Rates

The Gini and Theil results on total inequality and gendered inequality evolution for the six Asian and Latin American countries of our sample are presented in Table 7.3. It is important to stress that these results refer to the basic wage urban population. On the other hand when we look at the data of the table it is also worth to note that when we look at individual gender differences the magnitude of the index of inequality also diminishes. In the well known estimations of inequality form total household income the scale of inequality is higher because the marriage market is very homogamic in most of the countries. By definition, our data does not include the inequality shares of the top (owners and employers) and the bottom (poor and employed in the informal economy) of the income distribution. In spite of all these problems, by

Table 7.3 Inequality and gender in urban Latin America and East Asia

Country	Gini			Theil			Inequality		
							Within		Between
	Total	Men	Women	Total	Men	Women	Men (%)	Women (%)	%
Argentina 1975	0.026	0.176	0.226	0.098	0.065	0.084	51.18	19.94	28.87
Argentina 1985	0.266	0.252	0.26	0.119	0.104	0.123	51.91	42.24	5.84
Argentina 1995	0.262	0.266	0.251	0.111	0.118	0.1	66.23	33.61	0.16
Brasil 1976	0.406	0.418	0.421	0.275	0.234	0.288	60.44	30.24	9.33
Brasil 1999	0.367	0.378	0.341	0.216	0.23	0.187	68.78	30.76	0.45
Uruguay 1985	0.287	0.282	0.257	0.136	0.132	0.106	58.75	30.60	10.65
Uruguay 1995	0.284	0.278	0.282	0.128	0.123	0.126	57.55	39.70	2.75
Uruguay 1990	0.132	0.145	0.086	0.027	0.032	0.013	63.18	22.33	14.49
Uruguay 1997	0.14	0.124	0.084	0.03	0.025	0.013	49.45	16.89	33.66
Korea 1985	0.258	0.193	0.269	0.109	0.062	0.122	37.65	37.32	25.03
Korea 1995	0.156	0.125	0.122	0.039	0.024	0.027	39.79	24.80	35.41
Singapore 1985	0.254	0.264	0.238	0.113	0.111	0.103	63.94	32.04	4.02
Singapore 1995	0.244	0.238	0.24	0.098	0.098	0.096	60.15	39.51	0.34

Source See Part 2

Table 7.4 Gender gap evolution and dissimilarity index in a sample of urban Asian and Latin American countries, 1975–1995

Country	Year	Index dissimilarity	Gender gap (female/male earnings)
Argentina	1975	0.68	0.55
Argentina	1985	0.41	0.79
Argentina	1995	0.34	0.91
Brasil	1976	0.56	0.59
Brasil	1999	0.62	0.91
Uruguay	1985	0.54	0.70
Uruguay	1995	0.56	0.84
China	1990	0.35	0.84
China	1997	0.38	0.74
South Korea	1985	0.35	0.6
South Korea	1995	0.34	0.7
Singapore	1985	0.49	0.82
Singapore	1995	0.52	0.95

Source See Part 2 of the paper

studying urban waged labor we are able to identify some of the gender inequality patterns that arise from changes in the gender gap.

In Table 7.4, we present the evolution of the gender gap (or, to be more precise, the female/male earnings ratio) and index of dissimilarity for the six countries of our sample. The latter ranges from 0 to 1. When the dissimilarity index of occupations is close to 1 this means that occupations are more segregated according to gender than when the index is close to 0. This index quantifies the extent to which men and women can be substitutes in the labor market but it does not explain if the occupation segregation or its absence involves changes in income levels.

A first result we can stress from this table is that gender inequality has improved in all countries with the exception of China and South Korea in recent decades. In all Latin American countries, including Brasil, the gender gap has eroded from 1975 to 1995. Therefore from our case studies we can infer that in Latin America women's situation has improved a great deal. When we try to explain why, we must remember the results we got in the previous section: market openness reinforced by the existing catholic religion cultural backgrounds fostered the improvement of the human capital endowments of women.

Table 7.5 Female economic activity. World indicators

	Rate (% 2003) >15	Index (1990=100)	% of male rate
World	55.6	103	69
OECD	51.8	107	72
Developing countries	56.0	102	67
Arab States	33.3	119	42
East Asia and Pacific	68.9	100	83
Latin America	42.7	110	52
South Asia	44.1	107	52
Sub-Saharan Africa	62.3	99	73

Source: *Human Development Report* (2005, p. 314)

Table 7.6 Female literacy. World indicators, 2003

	Adult literacy		Youth literacy	
	Female rate >15	Female/male	Female rate 15–24	Female/male
Developing countries	69.6	84	81.2	92
Arab States	53.1	71	75.8	87
East Asia and Pacific	86.2	91	97. 5	99
Latin America	88.9	98	96.3	101
South Asia	46.6	66	63.3	79
Sub-Saharan Africa	52.6	76	67.9	88

Source: *Human Development Report* (2005, p. 310)

According to the index of dissimilarity more economic equality according to gender does not imply that women perform the same jobs than men. The indexes of dissimilarity are high and imply that women are employed in different occupations than men. We can also see in Tables 7.5 and 7.6 of this paper that women's participation levels are lower in Latin America than in East Asia. Indeed we have identified that Latin American working women from these 3 countries concentrate in the employment opportunities provided by liberal professions (teachers, nurses) clerical work (administrative) and services, and therefore the job and professional choices of women are different from those of men. This case is very significant on the importance of the freedom of choice and human capital achievements on the erosion of the gender gap. Notice that we must read the meaning of this information in terms of a trend and not in absolute terms. We already have stressed the limitations of our data that are the basic wage rates of urban workers. But there is no reason to expect that if gender differences narrow for this particular sector of the population other parts of the society are going to behave very differently. Of course globalization brought free trade to Latin America and together with it the growth of the informal sector of the economy. But as stated before the information we present here deals with the waged formal sector of the economy and still the real size and behavior of the informal sector is imprecise to reach conclusions.

The gender gap information arising from East Asian case is very different. Except for Singapore, gender economic inequality is higher in East Asia than in Latin America. The gender gap only slightly improves in the case of Singapore and worsens in the cases of South Korea and China. The Chinese case deserves special attention. Before the economic reforms that began in 1987, the wage distribution in this communist country was very egalitarian and inequality has specially increased after 1991 when the scale and scope of the economic reforms intensified (see the Chinese inequality patterns in Knight et al. 2001; Gustafsson and Shi 2001).

In Table 7.2, we have seen that in spite of the effects of market openness are to narrow the gender differences in countries with the cultural backgrounds of China and South Korea, in this particular cases religion is the engine that widens gender differences of these transition and capitalist economies of East Asia. On the other hand the dissimilarity index shows that in this case women's are less segregated. In this respect the Chinese example is illustrative. Urban women have very low fertility rates and they are present in the blue-collar spheres of the economy. In the case of China (like in most developing countries) real wages were very low because the productivity levels were also very low. The strategy has been to specialize in the production of export goods like textiles that make intensive use of the pool of cheap and unskilled female labor. By means of the production of labor intensive products, they could compete at the international markets. In these East Asian cases the causes of women's exclusion are not economic and as we have already stated the gender gap increases (both in terms of wage rate and in terms of human capital) because of cultural and religion reasons.

Therefore the direction of the move in Latin American countries is different from the East Asian case. In both cases there has been a trend toward market openness and globalization of trade. But the impact of culture and religion on gender differences has been very diverse. While economic planification was an instrument to level up the incomes of men and women in the past, market openness and exposure and freedom of choice has increased differences between men and women in Buddhist and Muslim countries as a consequence of gendered cultural backgrounds. The opposite effect can be found in Latin America. In this second case, trade competition with the cheap prices (and low wages) supplied by China has meant increasing economic inequality. But income and human capital gender gaps substantially narrowed. Freedom of choice has meant better health and education for women as well as for men and this fact has had as an effect the erosion of the human capital gender gap and as a consequence also the income gender gap.

Conclusions

In the previous pages we have presented the available comparative data on the gender gap and the factors that shape it. Market openness but also religious beliefs can explain the path toward a more egalitarian gender situation in Latin America as opposed to the gender regression in East Asia. The effects of globalization on freedom of choice and public visibility and empowerment of women have had clear outcomes on a better human capital formation of Latin American women and therefore on their economic performance. In this case we have also observed that the result obtained is positively influenced by the religion (and cultural backgrounds) practised in this part of the world which is Catholicism. But in other countries also experiencing globalization and the transition to the market economy such as countries from East Asia, we find the opposite effect. Here market openness also has a positive effect on the erosion of the gender gap. Nonetheless and in economic terms the point of departure of these transition economies was total equality of income distribution. The positive effects brought by market openness on the human capital gender gap are here eliminated by gendered religious beliefs and culture that repeal the effects of economic openness.

Once we tried to give here the general picture we must nevertheless stress the fact that to totally capture gender well-being and equality of opportunities in these two sets of countries more research is needed. We need to know more on women employed in the informal sector of the economy in Latin American countries and also we need to dig deeper on the effective inequality reality of East Asian women.

Bibliography

Alesina, A., Devleeschauer, A., Easterly, W., Kurlat, S., Wacziarg R., "Fractionalization", Mimeo, Harvard University, Economics Department, 2002.

Artecona, R., Cunningham, W., "Effects of Trade Liberalization on the Gender Wage Gap in Mexico", Working Paper, The World Bank Development Group, 2002.

Barro, R.J., Lee J.-W., "Data Set for a Panel of 138 Countries", 1994. Available from the National Bureau of Economic Research at www.nber.org/pub/barro.lee/zip.

Barro, R.J., Lee, J.-W., "International Measures of Schooling Years and Schooling Quality", *American Economic Review,* Papers and Proceedings, 86, no. 2 (1996): 218–223.

Barro, R.J., Lee, J.-W., "International Data on Educational Attainment Updates and Implications", Working Paper, Harvard University, August 2000.

Becker, G., *The Economics of Discrimination.* Chicago, University of Chicago Press, 1957.

Becker, G. et al., "Quantity and Quality of Life and World Inequality", *The American Economic Review*, 95, no. 1 (March 2005): 277–291.

Bertola, L., Williamson, J.G., "Globalisation in Latin America Before 1940", in *Cambridge Economic History of Latin America*, edited by V. Blumer-Thomas, J. Coatsworth, R. Cortes Conde. Cambridge, MA, Harvard, 2006.

Bloom, D., Williamson, J.G., "Demographic Transitions and Economic Miracles in Emerging Asia", *World Bank Economic Review* (September 1998): 419–455.

Blumer-Thomas, V. (ed.), *The New Economic Model in Latin America and Its Impact on Income Distribution and Poverty*. London, Institute of Latin American Studies, 1996.

Bourguignon, F., Morrison, C., "Income Distribution Among World Citizens: 1820–1990", *American Economic Review*, 92 (September 2002): 1113–1132.

Boserup, E., *Woman's Role in Economic Development*. Hants, Gower Publishing CL, 1970.

Chai, J.C.H., Chai, K.B., "Economic Reforms and Inequality in China", *Rvisita Internazionale di Szienze Economiche e Commerciali*, 41, no. 8 (1994): 675–696.

Chia-Yu Hung, "Over Education and Under Education in Taiwan", *Journal of Asian Economics*, 19, no. 2 (2008): 125–137.

Coatsworth, J.H., "Political Economy and Economic organization", in *Cambridge Economic History of Latin America*, vol. 1, chapter 7, edited by V. Blumer-Thomas, J. Coatsworth, R. Cortes Conde. Cambridge, MA, Harvard, 2006.

Coatsworth, J.H., Williamson, J.G., "The Roots of Latin American Protectionism: Looking Before the Great Depression", in *Integrating the Americas. FTAA and Beyond*, edited by A. Estevedordal, D. Rodrik, A.M. Taylor, A. Velasco. Cambridge, DRCLAS, Harvard University, 2004.

Coudourier, G., Gomez-Galvarriato, A., "La evolución de la participación laboral de las mujeres en la industria: una visión de largo plazo", *Economía Mexicana*, 13, no. 1 (2004): 63–104.

Deininger, K., Squire, L., "A New Data Set Measuring Income Inequality", *The World Bank Economic Review*, 10, no. 3 (September 1996): 565–591.

Deininger, K., Squire, L. "New Ways of Looking at Old Issues: Inequality and Growth", *Journal of Development Economics*, 57, no. 2 (1998): 259–288.

Dell, M., "Widening the Border: The Impact of Nafta on Female Labor Force Participation in Mexico", Oxford University Working Paper, December 2005.

Engerman, S., Sokoloff, K.L., "Factor Endowments, Inequality and Paths of Development Among New World Economies", NBER Working Paper No. 9259, 2002.

Engerman, S., Sokoloff, K.L., "Colonialism, Inequality, and Long-Run Paths of Development", NBER Working Paper No. 11057, 2005.

Field, E., "Entitled Work, Urban Property Rights and the Labor Supply in Peru", Harvard Working Paper, December 2003.

Field, E., "Early Marriage and Female Schooling in Bangladesh", Harvard Working Paper, November 2005.

Fishlow, A., Fiszbein, A., Ramos, L., "Distribuzao de Renda no Brasil e no Argentina: Uma Analise Comparativa", *Pesquisa e Plantejamento Economico*, 23, no. 1 (1993): 1–31.

Fogel, R.W., *The Escape from Hunger and Premature Death, 1700–2100*. Cambridge, Cambridge University Press, 2004.

Freeman, R.B., Oostendrop, R.H., "Wages Around the World: Pay Across Occupations and Countries", NBER Working Paper No. 8058, 2000a.

Freeman, R.B., Oostendrop, R.H., "Occupational Wages Around the World (OWW)". National Bureau of Economic Research, 2000b. Available at www.nber.org/oww/.

Galor, O., Weil, D.N., "The Gender Gap, Fertility and Growth", *The American Economic Review*, 98 (1996): 374–387.

Garcia-Cuellar, R., "Essays on the Effects of Trade and Location on the Gender Gap: A Study of the Mexican Labor Market", Doctoral Dissertation, Harvard University, Economics Department.

Gustafsson, B., Shi, L., "Economic Transformation and the Gender Earnings Gap in Urban China", in *China's Retreat from Equality*, edited by Carl Riskin, Zhao Renwei, Li Shi. New York, East Gate Book, 2001.

ILO Data Sets. www.ilo.org/public/english/bureau/stat/child/actrep/octing.htm.

Knight, J., Shi, L., Renwei, Z., "A Spatial Analysis of Wages and Incomes in Urban China: Divergent Means, Convergent Inequality", in *China's Retreat from Equality*, edited by Carl Riskin, Zhao Renwei, Li Shi. New York, East Gate Books, 2001.

Goldin, C., *Understanding the Gender Gap*. Oxford, Oxford University Press, 1990.

Hazan, M., Berdugo, B., "Child Labor, Fertility and Economic Growth", *The Economic Journal*, 112 (2004): 810–828.

Higgins, M., Williamson, J.G., "Explaining Inequality the World Round: Cohort Size, Kuznets Curves, and Openness", *Journal of Southeast Asian Studies*, 40 (2003), 268–302.

ILO, October Inquiry, Geneva, 1983–2003.

Lindert, P.H., Williamson, J.G. "Does Globalization Make the World More Unequal?", in *Globalization in Historical Perspective*, edited by M.D. Bordo, A.M. Taylor, J.G. Williamson. Chicago, London, NBER and University Chicago Press, 2003.

Mason, A., *Population Change and Economic Development in East Asia. Challenges Met, Opportunities Seized.* Stanford, Stanford University Press, 2001.

O'Rourke, K.H., Williamson, J.G., *Globalization and History.* Cambridge, MA, MIT Press, 1999.

Prados de la Escosura, L., "When Did Latin America Fall Behind? Evidence from Long-Run International Inequality", Universidad Carlos III de Madrid, Working Paper 04-66, December 2004.

Prados de la Escosura, L., "Growth, Inequality and Poverty in Latin América: Historical Evidence, Controlled Conjectures", Paper presented at the Conference The New Comparative Economic History in Honor of Jeffrey G. Williamson, Harvard University, November 4–5, 2005.

Psacharopoulos, G., Morley, S., Fiszbein, A., Lee, H., Word, B., "Poverty and Income Distribution in Latin America: The Story of the 1980s", Processed, Latin America and The Caribbean Technical Department, Washington, DC, World Bank, 1992.

Reimers, F (ed.), *Unequal Schools, Unequal Chances: The Challenges to Equal Opportunity in the Americas*, Cambridge, DRCLAS, Harvard University, 2000.

Riskin, C., Renwei, Z., Shi, L. (ed.), *China's Retreat from Equality.* New York, East Gate, 2001.

Sala-i-Martin, X., "The Disturbing 'Rise' of Global Income Inequality", NBER Working Paper, 2003.

Samuelson, P., "International Trade and the Equalization of Factor Prices", *The Economic Journal*, 58 (1948): 163–184.

Schultz, T.P., "Does the Liberalization of Trade Advance Gender Equality in Schooling and Health?" IZA Discussion Paper No. 2140, 2006.

Sen, A., "More Than 100 Million Women Are Missing", *The New York Review*, December 20, 1990.

Sen, A., "Missing Women: Social Inequality Outweighs Women's Survival Advantage in Asia and North Africa", *British Medical Journal*, 304 (March 7, 1992): 587–588.

Sen, A., "Missing Women-Revisited. Reduction in Female Mortality Has Been Counterbalanced by Sex Selective Abortions", *British Medical Journal*, 327 (December 6, 2003): 1297–1298.

Shi, L., Gustafsson, B., "Unemployment, Earlier Retirement, and Changes in the Gender Income Gap in Urban China, 1995–2002" in *Inequality and Public Policy in China*, edited by B.A. Gustafsson, Li Shi, Terry Sicular. Cambridge, Cambridge University Press, 2008.

Song Lee, B., Jang, S., Sarkar, J. "Women's Labor Force Participation and Marriage: The Case of Korea", *Journal of Asian Economics*, 19 (2008): 138–154.

Thorp, R., *Progress, Poverty and Exclusion: An Economic History of Latin America in the 20th Century*. New York, Inter-American Development Bank, 1998.

United Nations. *Human Development Report*. New York, 2005.

Wan, G., Ming, Lu, Chen, Zhao, "Globalization and Regional Income Inequality: Empirical Evidence from Within China", in *Understanding Inequality and Poverty in China: Methods and Applications*, edited by G. Wan. London, Palgrave Macmillan, 2008.

Williamson, J.G., "Globalization and Inequality, Past and Present", *World Bank Research Observer*, 12 (1997): 117–135.

World Bank, *World Development Report 1995: Workers in an Integrating World*. New York, Oxford University Press, 1995.

Wood, A., *North-South Trade, Employment and Inequality: Changing Fortunes in a Skill-Driven World*. Oxford: Clarendon Press, 1994.

Weichselbaumer, D., Winter-Ebmer, R., "The Effects of Competition and Equal Treatment Laws on the Gender Wage Differential", CEPR Discussion Paper Series No. 4015 Century, Inter-American Development Bank, New York, 2003.

8

Income and Human Capital Inequality and Ethnicity in the Americas During the Second Era of Globalization (1960–2010)

Abstract The aim of this chapter is to present the results on the impact of ethnicity on inequality, in terms of both income and educational achievement, in the Americas (North and South). It focuses on the period of the second era of globalization, from 1960 to 2010, before debates on Brexit in Europe and the adoption of protectionist economic policies in the United States. This period was chosen because of the intensification of international trade and interaction between North and South American countries. In this context, the chapter is specifically interested in the different implications of the racial composition of the labor force for inequality measures and employment. Although unequal opportunity between blacks, whites, and indigenous peoples narrowed over the period, greater public efforts are needed to fully achieve equal opportunity.

Keywords Race · Ethnicity · Globalization · Inequality · Economic growth

E. Camps-Cura, *Changes in Population, Inequality and Human Capital Formation in the Americas in the Nineteenth and Twentieth Centuries*, Palgrave Studies in Economic History, https://doi.org/10.1007/978-3-030-21351-0_8

Introduction

Among the most pressing motivations to write this chapter there is the fact that by the end of the twentieth century Latin America was, with no doubt or discussion the most unequal continent of the world (in terms of income) after Africa. On the other hand, and regarding ethnicity, recent literature stresses that in North America racial differences have narrowed in the recent past (while still existing), but more evidence is needed for Latin America and the Caribbean. Research on South and Central America is not yet clear on the outcomes of ethnic and racial differences and its impact on educational and income inequality.

In this chapter, we try to show the relationship between race and ethnicity and inequality in the Americas and further implications. The time period under study, 1960–2010, has been chosen since it represents the first stage of the second era of globalization, in spite of the financial crisis. We finish by 2010 or before, since after this date the United States adopted protectionist policies, but before the Americas, North and South, were strongly interacting.

On the recent literature on these topics, we must go back to the introductory Chapter 1 where we presented a summary of the most relevant literature on income and educational inequality in the long run. From the authors quoted there, and concerning implications for the study of the second era of globalization we want to remember the following. On the one hand the work by Acemoglu et al. (2002) and Acemoglu and Robinson (2012) on the role of the economic and political institutions in the Americas. According to these authors while institutions are and have been inclusive in the United States, leading to the early establishment of a Democratic Constitution, economic cooperation, and political freedom, institutions of Latin America are and have been extractive, leading to the concentration of power by a white elite that look at the maximum extraction of goods and commodities from mines and plantations. These institutions cause that levels of per capita GDP, welfare expenditure in health and education are much lower in

South America than in the North. According to these authors, the origins of this divergence go back to the colonial period, and the different colonial policies implemented by the British and other North European powers in North America with respect to policies implemented by the Iberian metropolis in South America.

Engerman and Sokoloff (2012) do not totally agree with Acemoglu and Robinson stressing that institutions are part of the social capital of a country and that therefore they are endogenous to the economic performance. According to these authors, the main exogenous cause explaining inequality in Latin America is the concentration of production factors (land, labor, and capital) in a few hands. The iberian white elite was always a minority of the total population owning big plantations and mines that made intensive use of capital, land, and labor in each economic settlement. The institutions stemming from these economic exogenous variables are the limitation of the access to education to the white population, the limitation of the right to vote to the literate population (therefore the whites), and the limitation of the access to property to the white elite. According to Engerman and Sokoloff (2012), the situation was very different in the United States where production factors were much less concentrated and this led soon to the spread of more democratic institutions regarding education, the right to vote, and access to property. According to these authors, the same as for Acemoglu and Robinson, the reasons behind the different inequality levels in North and South Americas go back to the colonial period and the different economic policies implemented by the colonial powers.

Finally Williamson (2010, 2015) disagree with the authors quoted till now stressing that during the colonial period levels of per capita GDP were to low to allow for inequality and in any case inequality was not higher than the levels achieved in Europe and other parts of the world. Latin American and Caribbean countries' inequality rose with the first globalization era (1870–1914) and after that lost the leveling impact of the Golden Age in most countries. Therefore Latin America has become the most unequal continent in the world only in the recent past.

Data Sources and Methodology

To measure income inequality we made use of public of Gini coefficients, published by Prados de la Escosura (2007) for some Latin American countries and World Bank Datasets for the rest of countries. Data on Gini Coefficients of educational inequality are available at Clio Infra Dataset and are part of the Maddison Project led by Jan Luiten van Zanden. Data on ethnicity for the year 2000 come from Alesina et al. Publication (2003) and for the year 1960 from Rosenblat (1945). Control variables on geography come from Acemoglu et al. (2002). Data on the economic sector of employment come from Clio Infra Dataset, World Bank, and Barro and Lee. Data on education come from Barro and Lee (2013) and data on per capita GDP are from the Maddison project.

In order to obtain results on the impact of race on GDP per capita and education we made a simple cross section OLS analysis. We obtain the result that there is a low change of race over the short run to justify a panel or longitudinal analysis. The results on economic inequality and educational inequality according to race involve all countries with available data. We first present the results of all countries with their name and after the fitted results of income inequality and educational inequality weighted by the country's population size. In order to fit the results we used linear, quadratical, and power functions. Finally we also present the main sectors of employment according to race. The fitted results are also weighted by the country's population size.

Results on Ethnicity, Education, and Economic Growth

In Tables 8.1, 8.2, 8.3, and 8.4 we present a regression analysis on the impact of ethnicity on GDP per capita and years of education in Latin American Countries with available data, using geographical data by Acemoglu et al. (2002) as control variables. As you can observe, one of the limitations of this analysis is the number of observations, around 20, since the results are obtained at the country level for all Latin American countries with available data and with a similar size. Extremely small countries were excluded from our analysis. Nonetheless, and in spite of the low number of observations, we obtain statistically significant results.

The main finding from Tables 8.1, 8.2, 8.3, and 8.4 is that while ethnic differences have narrowed over the last decades, particularly in North America, the results are different for Latin American and Caribbean countries. In this second group of countries, being black has a negative impact on per capita GDP and years of education; being white has a positive impact; and being indigenous correlates to an intermediate position. On the other hand, in Table 8.5 we present

Table 8.1 GDP per capita and ethnicity (1960)

	(1)	(2)	(3)	(4)
Black	−0.006	−0.006	−0.006	0.002
	(0.006)	(0.006)	(0.006)	(0.008)
White	0.008**	0.009*	0.008*	0.007*
	(0.004)	(0.005)	(0.004)	(0.004)
Indian	0.001	−0.000	0.001	−0.001
	(0.007)	(0.007)	(0.007)	(0.007)
Asian	−0.034	−0.047	−0.035	−0.074
	(0.114)	(0.128)	(0.127)	(0.115)
Abs(latitude of capital)/90		−0.188		
		(1.412)		
Temperature: average			0.000	
			(0.023)	
=1 if landlocked				−0.382
				(0.374)
=1 if island				−0.865
				(0.531)
Constant	7.624***	7.679***	7.616***	7.782***
	(0.236)	(0.336)	(0.491)	(0.243)
Observations	20	19	20	19
Adjusted R^2	0.198	0.136	0.141	0.287

Standard errors in parentheses. The dependent variable is the logarithm of GDP per capita in 1960. The omitted category for race variables is the proportion of mixed population

$^*p<0.1$, $^{**}p<0.05$, $^{***}p<0.01$

Table 8.2 GDP per capita and ethnicity (2000)

	(1)	(2)	(3)	(4)
Black	−0.014**	−0.014**	−0.014**	−0.015
	(0.006)	(0.006)	(0.006)	(0.008)
White	0.010**	0.010*	0.010**	0.009**
	(0.004)	(0.004)	(0.004)	(0.004)
Indian	0.002	0.001	0.002	0.002
	(0.007)	(0.007)	(0.007)	(0.007)
Asian	0.101	0.093	0.104	0.095
	(0.115)	(0.125)	(0.128)	(0.123)
Abs(latitude of capital)/90		0.262		
		(1.373)		
Temperature: average			−0.001	
			(0.023)	
=1 if landlocked				−0.404
				(0.401)
=1 if island				−0.044
				(0.569)
Constant	8.066***	8.077***	8.091***	8.169***
	(0.237)	(0.326)	(0.492)	(0.260)
Observations	20	19	20	19
Adjusted R^2	0.465	0.443	0.427	0.443

Standard errors in parentheses. The dependent variable is the logarithm of GDP per capita in 2000. The omitted category for race variables is the proportion of mixed population
$^{*}p<0.1$, $^{**}p<0.05$, $^{***}p<0.01$

the impact of ethnicity on economic growth. We see that the interannual GDP per capita growth rate (1960–2010) of countries with a proportion of 60% or more of white population is pretty high (1.98%) and more than double the rate of growth of countries with 40% or more of black and mixed population (0.89%). Finally countries with more than 60% of indigenous or mixed population obtain an intermediate position (1.71%). The rate of growth of countries with a majority of indigenous and mixed populations is nonetheless relatively high (only 0.17% lower than the growth of countries with a majority of white population) showing gains in growth achieved by indigenous population during this period in which indigenous leaders began to implement populist policies. Even if the limits of such policies is

Table 8.3 Average years of education and ethnicity (1960)

	(1)	(2)	(3)	(4)
Black	−0.010	−0.010	−0.008	−0.004
	(0.008)	(0.008)	(0.010)	(0.011)
White	0.029***	0.025***	0.029***	0.031***
	(0.006)	(0.0 06)	(0.006)	(0.006)
Indian	0.022**	0.024**	0.021**	0.018*
	(0.009)	(0.0 09)	(0.009)	(0.009)
Asian	0.405**	0.498**	0.432**	0.368**
	(0.177)	(0.175)	(0.197)	(0.170)
Abs(latitude of capital)/90		3.236		
		(1.896)		
Temperature: average			−0.014	
			(0.041)	
=1 if landlocked				1.144*
				(0.549)
=1 if island				−0.214
				(0.764)
Constant	1.862***	1.336**	2.134**	1.726***
	(0.357)	(0.456)	(0.862)	(0.355)
Observations	20	20	20	20
Adjusted R^2	0.641	0.682	0.619	0.690

Standard errors in parentheses. The dependent variable is the average years of education (1960). The omitted category for race variables is the proportion of mixed population
$*p<0.1$, $**p<0.05$, $***p<0.01$

evidenced in the present, in its first stage, in countries such as Mexico and Perú (and others) it attained a relative success. Therefore, from results presented in Tables 8.1, 8.2, 8.3, 8.4, and 8.5 we can confirm that ethnicity and the racial composition of the population had a high impact on human capital formation, at least on education and economic growth, even during the second era of globalization. This results square well with the thesis presented by Engerman and Sokoloff (2012)—see the introduction of this chapter—regarding the existence of an elite composed of white population in Latin American and Caribbean countries, which had more access to education and therefore more impact and success on economic growth while black or mixed population had an opposite situation, with fewer

Table 8.4 Average years of education and ethnicity (2000)

	(1)	(2)	(3)	(4)
Black	−0.022	−0.020	−0.017	−0.013
	(0.015)	(0.015)	(0.018)	(0.022)
White	0.027**	0.015	0.021*	0.020
	(0.010)	(0.011)	(0.011)	(0.012)
Indian	0.025	0.023	0.018	0.016
	(0.017)	(0.016)	(0.017)	(0.019)
Asian	0.330	0.705**	0.619	0.529
	(0.289)	(0.326)	(0.354)	(0.348)
Abs(latitude of capital)/90		4.644		
		(3.530)		
Temperature: average			−0.025	
			(0.074)	
=1 if landlocked				−0.239
				(1.123)
=1 if island				−0.890
				(1.562)
Constant	6.068***	4.342***	5.580***	5.249***
	(0.596)	(0.850)	(1.548)	(0.725)
Observations	20	20	20	20
Adjusted R^2	0.410	0.328	0.252	0.211

Standard errors in parentheses. The dependent variable is the average years of education (2000). The omitted category for race variables is the proportion of mixed population
$*p<0.1$, $**p<0.05$, $***p<0.01$

Table 8.5 Average GDP per capita growth (1960–2010) by ethnic composition

Ethnic composition	Average interannual GDP p.c. growth rate (1960–2010) (%)
Above 60% white	1.89
Above 40% black or mixed	0.89
Above 60% Indian or mixed	1.71

Note Above 60% white: Argentina, Chile, Costa Rica and Uruguay; above 40% black or mixed: Brazil, Cuba, Dominican Republic, Haiti, Nicaragua, Panama, Venezuela; above 60% indian or mixed: Bolivia, Colombia, Ecuador, El Salvador, Guatemala, Honduras, Mexico, Paraguay and Peru

years of education and a lower impact on per capita GDP and economic growth. Engerman and Sokoloff referred their results to the long run till the first half of the nineteenth century. In this part of this chapter, we see that those results have application till the recent past at least for Latin American and Caribbean countries.

Results on Ethnicity, Inequality, and Sector of Employment

Regarding the results on income and educational inequality in the following figures, we can verify that they were much higher in South and Central America than in North America. When we control these results by ethnicity we see that the United States and Canada, with a high proportion of whites, have lower levels on income inequality, with the significant exception of Cuba, that stands as the country with lower income Ginis. The highest levels are obtained in Brazil, with a significant proportion of whites, and Mexico with a low proportion of whites. When we look at the quadratically adjusted function in Fig. 8.2 we can see that Brazil and other LACs such as Chile, Costa Rica, Uruguay, and Argentina, with a high proportion of white population are outliers. The quadratical functions we fit are adjusted according to the population size. We can observe that the function is concave and clearly proves that the higher the proportion of white population the lower the levels of income Gini with the exception of Cuba.

The influence of being white on educational equality is even higher and here our fitted function clearly shows the effect that a higher proportion of white population has on the diminution of the educational Gini. LACs from the Southern Cone that had received an important population influx of European population also have low levels of educational inequality. As a general remark, we can say that the migrant population that these countries received since the late nineteenth century was more educated than natives, and this fact had a positive impact on the educational achievement of the future generations till the period we represent here. Countries with a higher proportion of indigenous, black, or mixed population have higher levels of educational inequality because they experienced to a lesser extent the positive effect on educational achievement of European immigration. These are countries where the quality of education is low, educational supply is segregated, and the basic elements to provide education (teachers, books, classrooms) have a deficit (see Chapter 2).

If we concentrate on the results of the fitted functions of income Ginis in the case of indigenous and blacks we see a nearly flat evolution with the increase of the share of indigenous population, and an increasing function in the case of black or mixed population. Countries with a high proportion of blacks (Brazil, Mexico, Colombia, Honduras) are those where the levels of income and educational inequality are higher. In addition the adjusted functions on the sector of employment show that they are mainly employed in agriculture, where we find a positive adjusted correlation, while in the case of industry and services the adjusted correlation is negative. This last fact may also explain why inequality in countries with a large share of black population is also higher. Blacks are mainly employed in the primary sector of the economy in firms such as big plantations receiving low salaries as a reward of their work. We therefore think that in South and Central America more efforts are needed to achieve equal opportunity between black and non-black population as we already presented in the previous regressions. In this case, inequality and economic specialization have further consequences on a lower path of economic growth.

See Figs. 8.1, 8.2, 8.3, 8.4, 8.5, 8.6, 8.7, 8.8, 8.9, 8.10, 8.11, 8.12, 8.13, 8.14, 8.15, 8.16, 8.17, 8.18, 8.19, 8.20, 8.21, 8.22, 8.23, and 8.24.

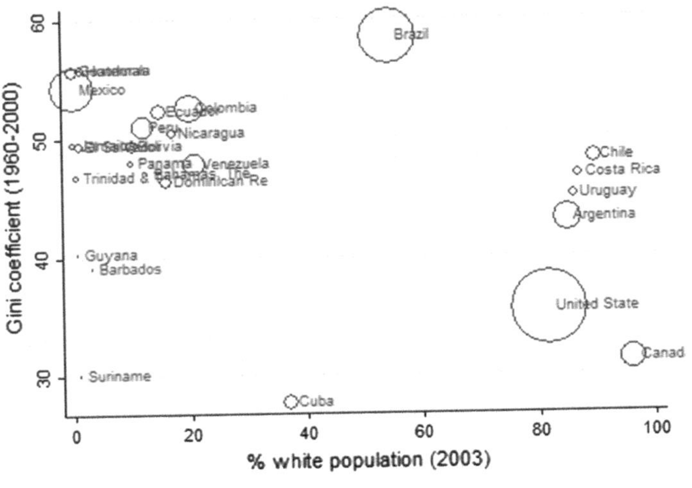

Fig. 8.1 Income inequality and white population (American countries, 1960–2005)

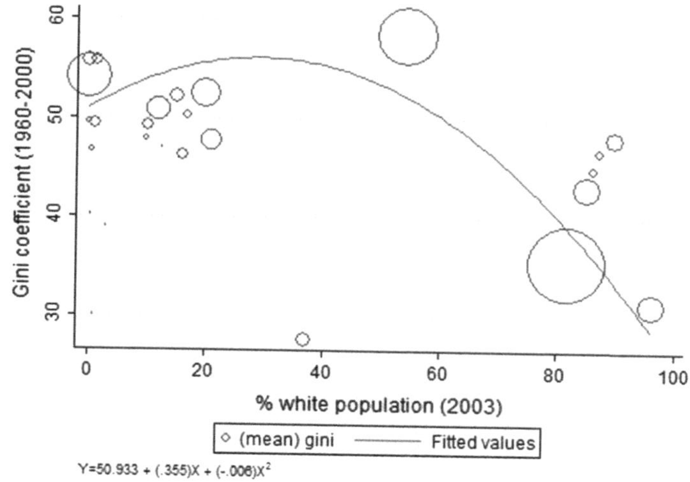

Fig. 8.2 Income inequality and white population (American countries, 1960–2005)

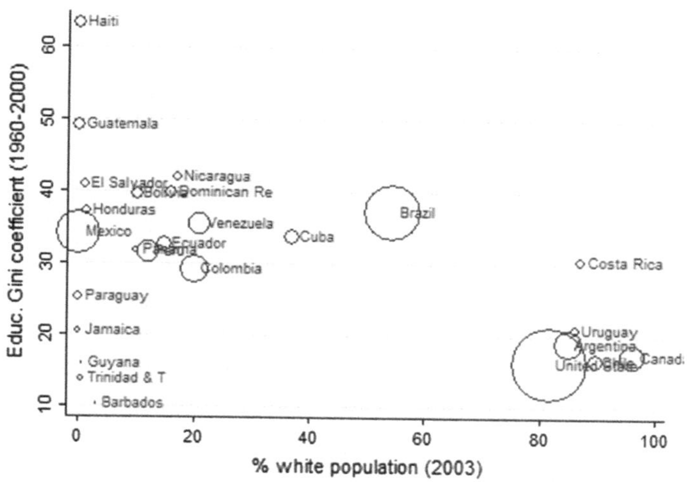

Fig. 8.3 Educational inequality and white population (American countries, 1960–2005)

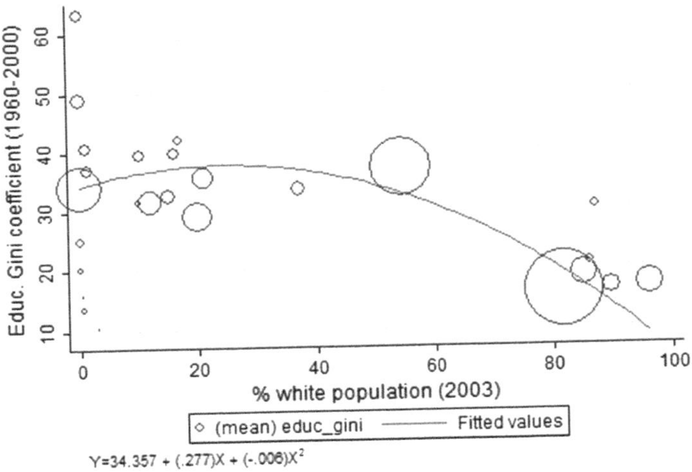

Fig. 8.4 Educational inequality and white population (American countries, 1960–2005)

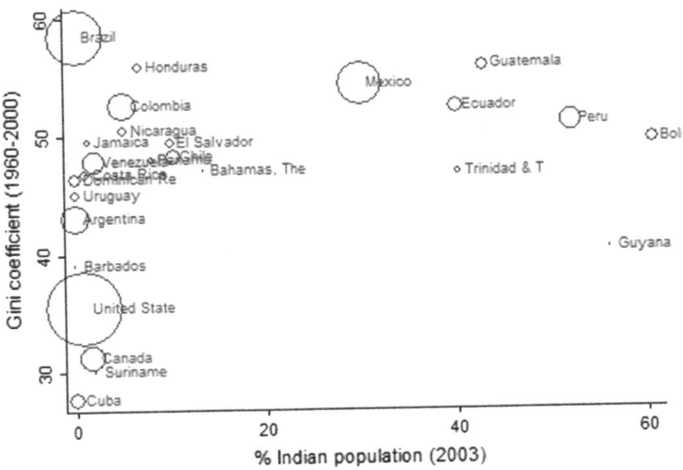

Fig. 8.5 Income inequality and Indian population (American countries, 1960–2005)

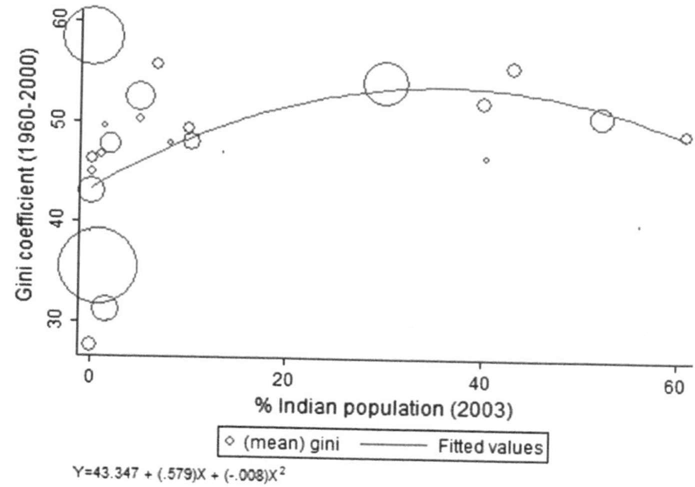

Fig. 8.6 Income inequality and Indian population (American countries, 1960–2005)

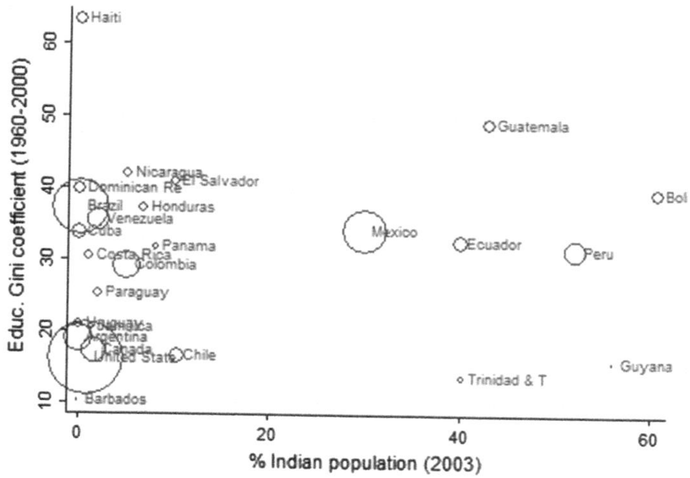

Fig. 8.7 Educational inequality and Indian population (American countries, 1960–2005)

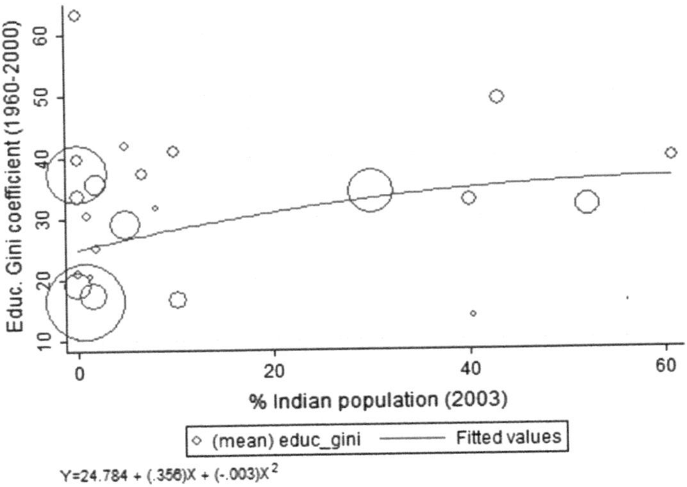

Fig. 8.8 Educational inequality and Indian population (American countries, 1960–2005)

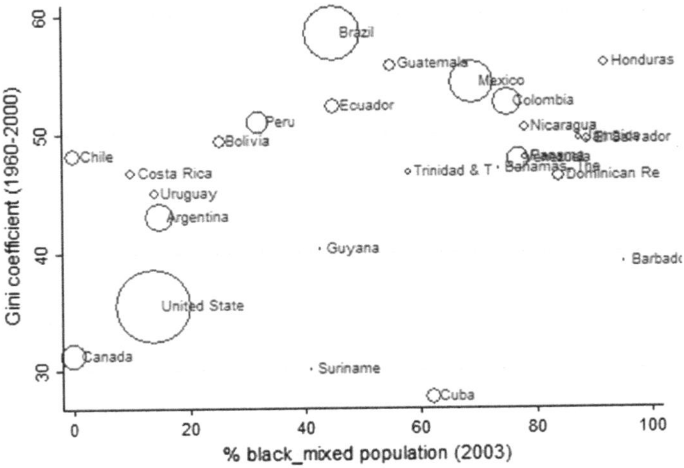

Fig. 8.9 Income inequality and black or mixed population (American countries, 1960–2005)

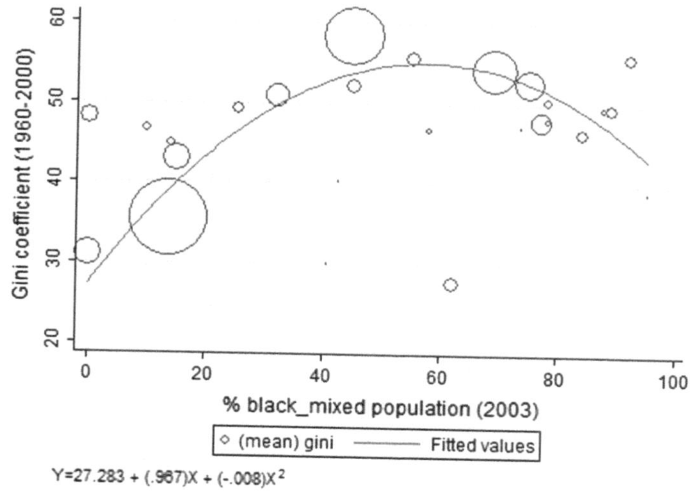

Fig. 8.10 Income inequality and black or mixed population (American countries, 1960–2005)

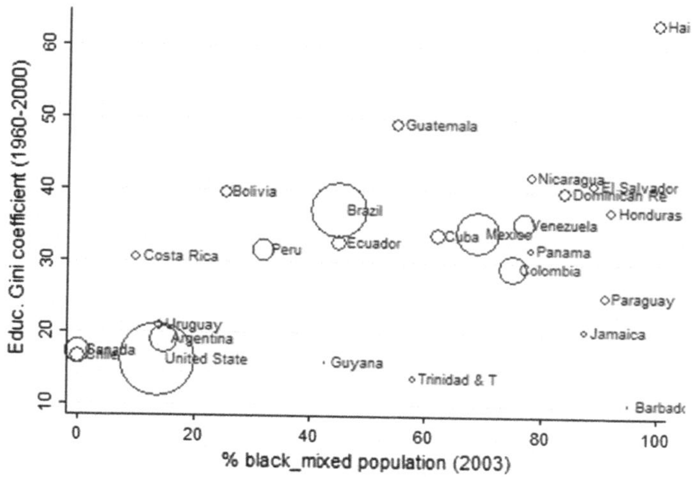

Fig. 8.11 Educational inequality and black or mixed population (American countries, 1960–2005)

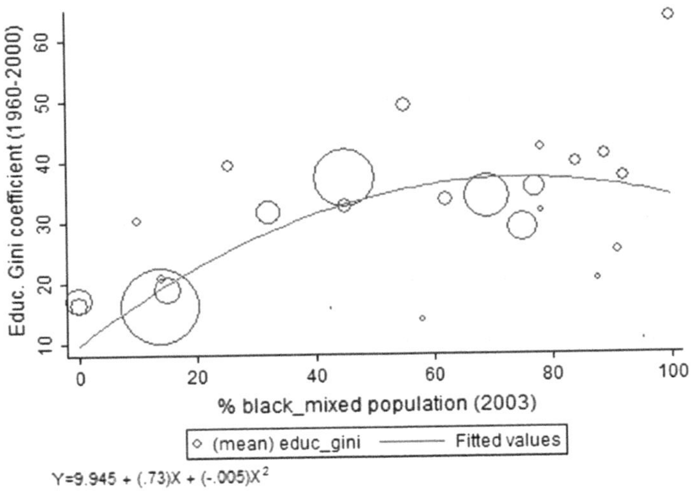

Fig. 8.12 Educational inequality and black or mixed population (American countries, 1960–2005)

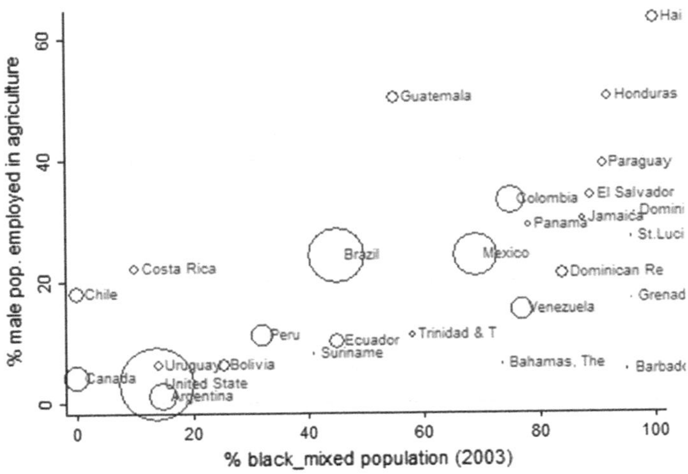

Fig. 8.13 Agricultural sector and black or mixed population (American countries, 1960–2005)

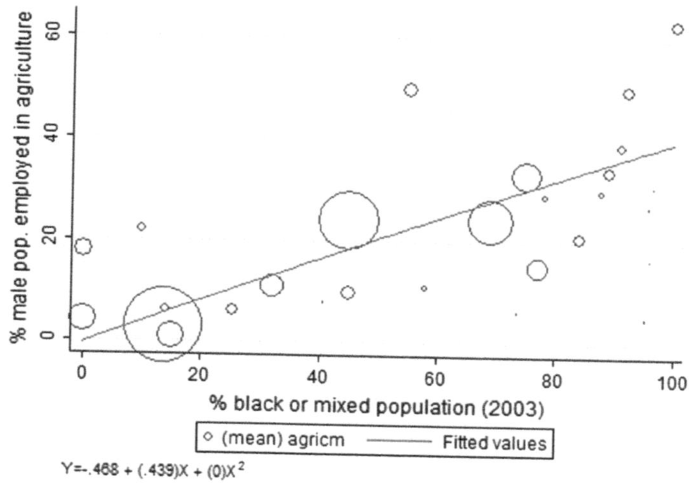

Fig. 8.14 Agricultural sector and black or mixed population (American countries, 1960–2005)

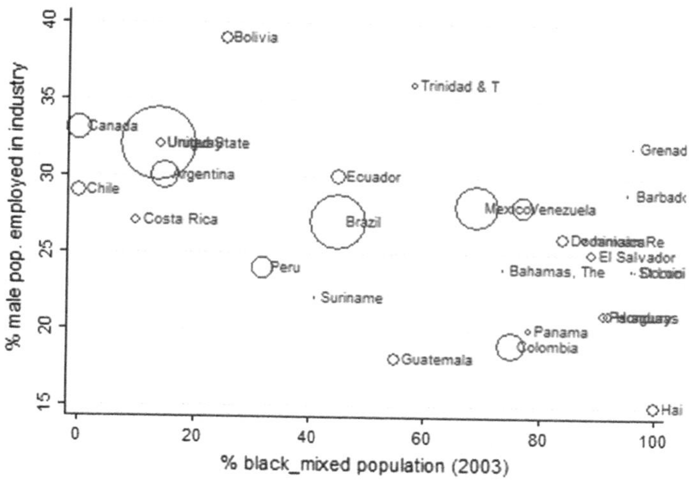

Fig. 8.15 Industrial sector and black or mixed population (American countries, 1960–2005)

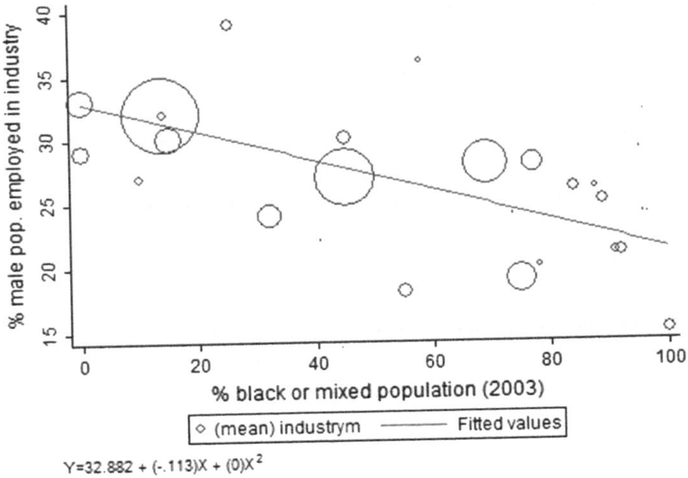

Fig. 8.16 Industrial sector and black or mixed population (American countries, 1960–2005)

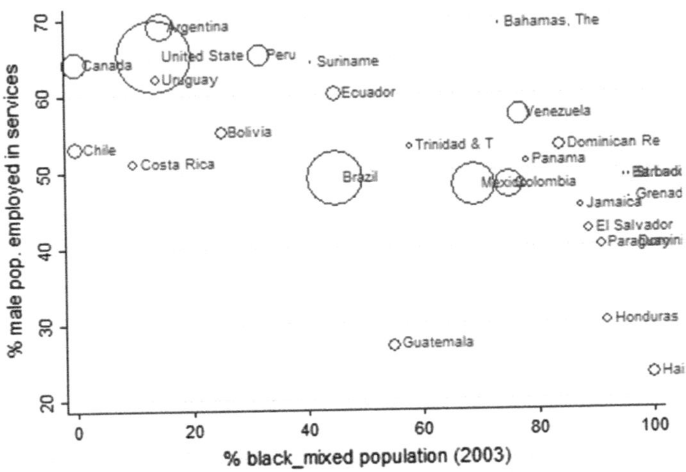

Fig. 8.17 Services sector and black or mixed population (American countries, 1960–2005)

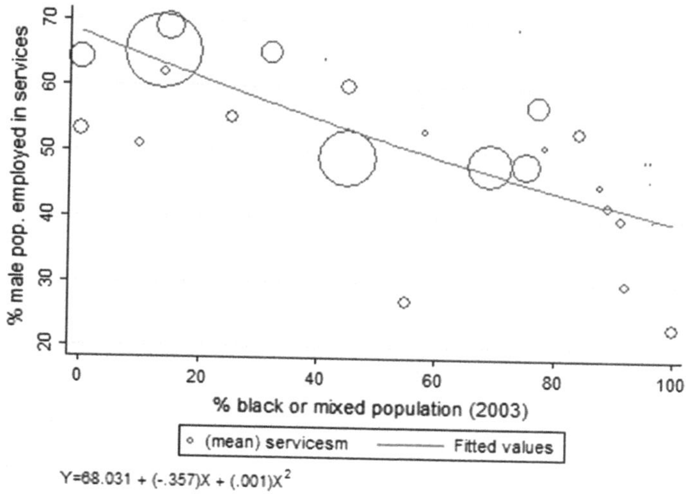

Fig. 8.18 Services sector and black or mixed population (American countries, 1960–2005)

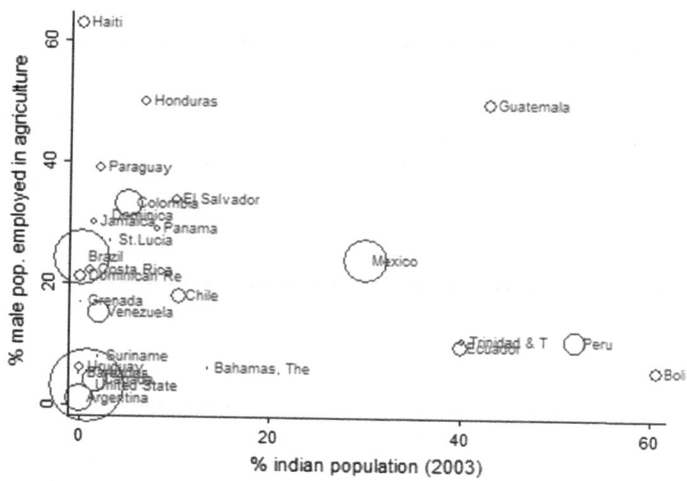

Fig. 8.19 Agricultural sector and Indian population (American countries, 1960–2005)

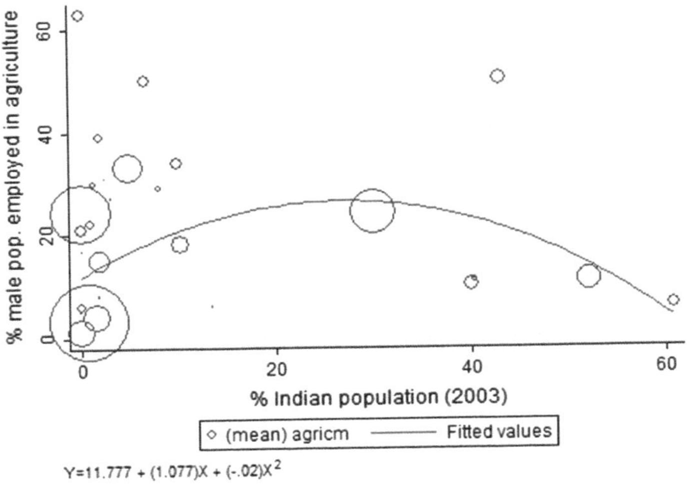

Fig. 8.20 Agricultural sector and Indian population (American countries, 1960–2005)

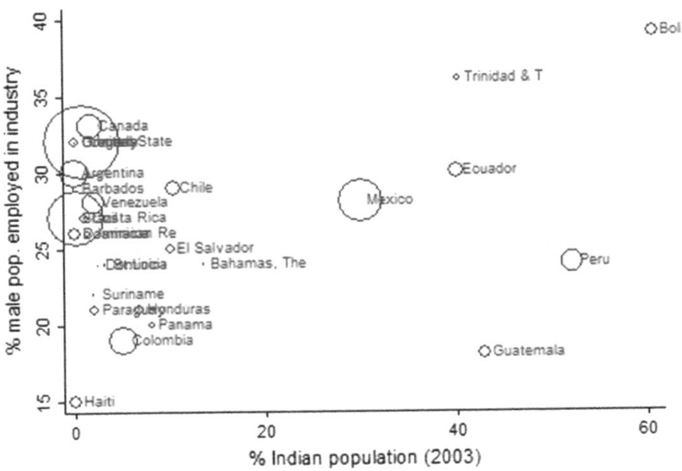

Fig. 8.21 Industrial sector and Indian population (American countries, 1960–2005)

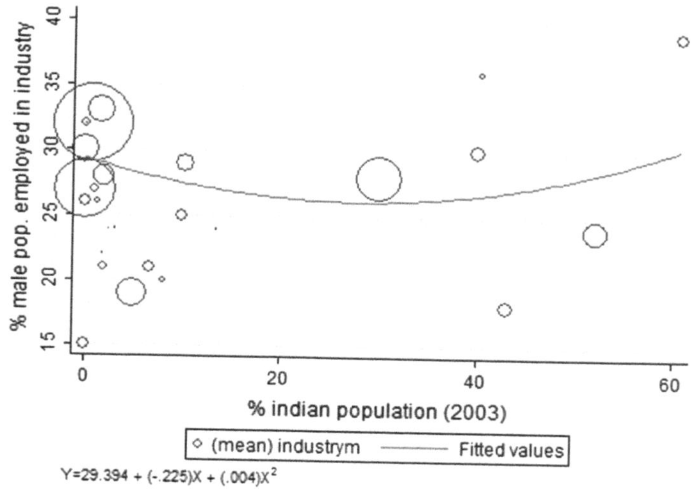

Fig. 8.22 Industrial sector and Indian population (American countries, 1960–2005)

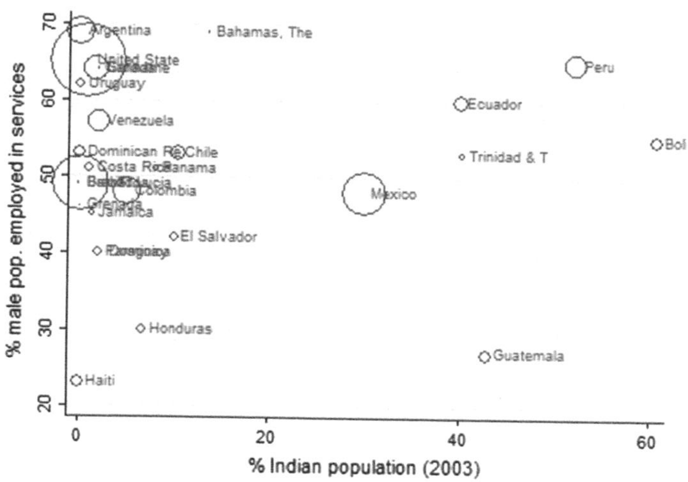

Fig. 8.23 Services sector and Indian population (American countries, 1960–2005)

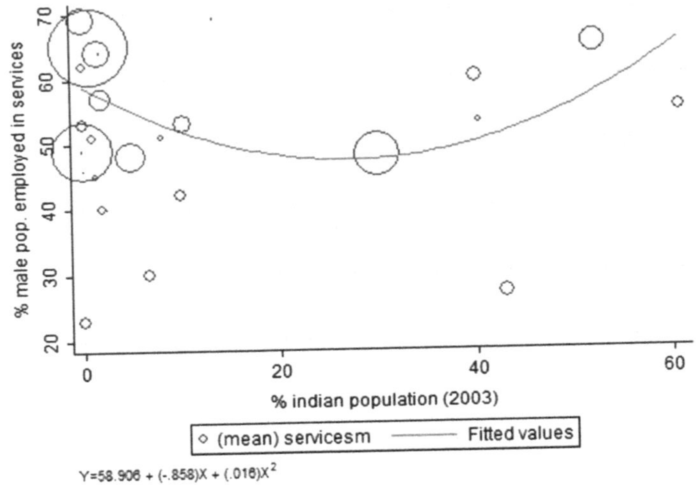

Fig. 8.24 Services sector and Indian population (American countries, 1960–2005)

Bibliography

Acemoglu, D., Johnson, S., Robinson, J.A., "Reversal of Fortune: Geography and Institutions in the Making of the Modern World Income Distribution", *The Quarterly Journal of Economics*, 117, no. 4 (November 1, 2002): 1231–1294.

Acemoglu, D., Robinson, J.A., *Why Nations Fail? The Origins of Power, Prosperity and Poverty*. New York, Crown Business, 2012.

Alesina, A., Easterly, W., Devleeschauwer, A., Kurlat, S., Wacziarg, R.T., "Fractionalization", *Journal of Economic Growth*, VIII (2003): 155–194.

Barro, R.J., Lee, J.W., "A New Data Set of Educational Attainment in the World, 1950–2010", *Journal of Development Economics*, 104C (2013): 184–198.

Engerman, S.L., Sokoloff, K.L., *Economic Development in the Americas Since 1500: Endowments and Institutions*. New York: Cambridge University Press and NBER, 2012.

Prados de la Escosura, L., "Inequality and Poverty in Latin America: A Long-Run Exploration", in *The New Comparative Economic History*, edited by T. Hatton, K. O'Rourke, A.M. Taylor. Cambridge, MA, MIT Press, 2007, pp. 291–315.

Rosenblat, A., *La población indígena en América desde 1942 hasta la actualidad.* Buenos Aires, Instituto de Filología de Buenos Aires, 1945.
Williamson J.G., "Five Centuries of Latin American Inequality", *Revista de Historia Económica, Journal of Iberian and Latin American Economic History,* 28, no. 2 (2010): 227–252.
Williamson, J.G., "Latin American Inequality: Colonial Origins, Commodity Booms or a Missed Twentieth Century Leveling", *Journal of Human Development and Capabilities,* 16, no. 3 (2015): 324–341.
World Bank Datasets. http://databank.worldbank.org.

Index

B

Biased 33, 34, 55
Blacks 15, 18, 19, 21–23, 52, 54, 55, 68, 70, 142

C

Capital 32, 34–36, 65, 89, 91, 95, 110, 135
Children 3, 14, 16, 18, 34, 35, 42, 43, 51, 52, 54, 55, 63, 68, 88–96, 100, 103–105, 110, 111
Culture 43, 51, 64, 95, 115, 116, 120, 127, 128

D

Demand 4, 34, 35, 88, 89, 93, 95, 112
Demographic transition 3, 36, 44, 45, 51, 88
Domestic 51, 95, 118

E

Education 2, 3, 6, 10–12, 14–18, 20, 22, 23, 26, 32–35, 37, 42, 45, 51, 52, 54, 55, 58, 59, 62–72, 75, 79, 88–93, 103–105, 111, 120, 122, 127, 134–137, 139–141
Endogenous 50, 51, 54, 62, 65, 89, 90, 135

E. Camps-Cura, *Changes in Population, Inequality and Human Capital Formation in the Americas in the Nineteenth and Twentieth Centuries*, Palgrave Studies in Economic History, https://doi.org/10.1007/978-3-030-21351-0

Ethnicity 10, 16, 18, 20, 52, 63, 69, 134, 136, 141
Exogenous 2, 50–52, 54, 62, 135

F
Fertility 42–46, 49–52, 54, 55, 57–59, 89–94, 100, 105, 126

G
Gap 5, 13, 16, 20, 23, 26, 52, 55, 92, 96, 100, 111–114, 116–120, 122, 124, 126–128
Gender 18, 33, 35, 52, 55, 64, 90, 92, 96, 100, 103, 110–120, 122, 124–128
Gini 3, 10, 32, 66–68, 96, 110, 111, 114, 116, 122, 136, 141
Globalization 2–4, 32, 36, 37, 58, 94, 95, 110–112, 120, 122, 126, 127, 134, 135, 139
Growth 4–6, 15, 33–36, 38, 39, 42–46, 50, 51, 54, 62–65, 68, 70, 71, 75, 89, 91, 93–95, 100, 103, 105, 110, 126, 136, 138–140, 142

H
Human capital 2, 14, 15, 33–35, 37–39, 51, 54, 62, 64, 65, 68, 69, 88, 89, 91–96, 100, 103, 104, 110–112, 115, 116, 118–120, 122, 124, 126–128, 139

I
Income 2, 3, 10, 16–18, 20, 22, 23, 26, 32, 34, 35, 37, 38, 43, 49, 52, 54, 59, 62–64, 66, 75, 88, 90, 92, 94–96, 100, 104, 110–120, 122, 124, 127, 128, 134, 136, 141, 142
Indian 21, 22, 54, 55, 69
Inequality 2–4, 6, 10, 11, 16–18, 20–23, 26, 32–38, 58, 63, 70, 92, 94, 96, 100, 110–117, 119, 120, 122, 124, 126–128, 134–136, 141, 142

L
Labour 32–39, 110, 112, 118, 124, 126, 135
Leveling 4, 33, 135
Life expectancy 44, 65, 68
Literacy 10, 11, 27, 33, 34, 44, 58, 59, 64, 65, 92

M
Market 4, 5, 37, 89, 90, 93, 104, 111, 112, 116, 118–120, 122, 124, 126–128
Mass migration 19, 20, 32

N
Native-Americans 19, 21, 23, 70
Non-whites 10, 15, 18
Numeracy 34

P

Productivity 14, 32, 34, 35, 38, 39, 88, 89, 115, 126
Public 3, 14, 15, 33, 35, 51, 52, 54, 96, 110, 127, 136

R

Race 10, 18–21, 35, 52, 54, 61, 63, 69, 70, 134, 136
Religion 43, 95, 120, 124, 126, 127
Rural 10–12, 15, 16, 64, 69, 88, 90, 116

S

Schooling 12–16, 18, 21–23, 37, 54, 58, 64, 65, 69, 70, 72, 103
Segmentation 14, 16, 20, 63, 69
Skill 15, 18, 33, 34, 62, 63, 88
Supply 3, 4, 20, 32, 34–36, 51, 52, 54, 63, 69, 88, 110, 118, 120, 141

T

Teachers 16, 125, 141
Technological change 5, 33, 34
Theil 32, 114, 116, 117, 122

U

Urban 10, 16, 64, 67, 69, 88, 90, 110, 113, 114, 116, 122, 124, 126

W

Work 17, 44, 51, 52, 88, 90, 92, 93, 95, 96, 100, 112, 113, 118, 120, 125, 134, 142

The manufacturer's authorised representative in the EU is Springer
Nature Customer Service Centre GmbH, Europaplatz 3, 69115 Heidelberg,
Germany. If you have any concerns regarding our products, please
contact ProductSafety@springernature.com

Printed and bound by CPI Group (UK) Ltd, Croydon, CR0 4YY
22/09/2026
02221063-0009